HILTON HEAD ISLAND:

Ebb & Flow

Edited by:

MIHO KINNAS
JAMES A. MALLORY
SANSING MCPHERSON
BILL NEWBY

Island Writers' Network
HILTON HEAD ISLAND, SOUTH CAROLINA

A project of
The Island Writers' Network
Hilton Head Island, SC
www.islandwritersnetworkhhi.org

ISBN-10: 1979272735
ISBN-13: 978-1979272735

Printed in the United States of America
First Printing

Dedication

To Elizabeth Robin
Island Writers' Network Moderator
2015 – 2017

Whose leadership, enthusiasm, and networking
have firmly established IWN's presence
in the Arts Community

Acknowledgements

This fifth anthology by the Island Writers' Network is the product of fifty writers and artists, all either permanent, part-time, or former residents of the Lowcountry; and all are in love with it.

We are indebted to our own members for their generosity, talent, and perseverance in polishing and editing their pieces. We greatly appreciate the members of the Camera Club of Hilton Head Island, the Photography Club of Beaufort, the Art League of Hilton Head, and the Photography Club of Sun City Hilton Head who generously offered photos for this anthology. Since a picture may be worth a thousand words, this volume is a perfect melding of both.

We wish to acknowledge those who have been of great assistance to the editorial team: Norma Van Amberg, proofreading; Thelma Naylor, document management; and Elizabeth Robin, thematic organization.

We also want to thank David Russell, our book designer, and the Heritage Library, our host over the eighteen years of IWN's existence.

The Editorial Board

Table of Contents

Side-Swiped!

The Funny Side

The Far Side

Taking a Side

The InSide Info

Side-Swiped

Donna Varner

Editors' Note: Hurricane Matthew hit Hilton Head Island on Saturday, October 8, 2016, as a Category2 storm, the first hurricane to hit this island since 1911. The trees—broken, tumbled and tossed.

Hurricane Matthew's selective destruction left one neighbor with a tree through his roof and another with nothing more than branches to clear from the yard. Still others found no water and sewer service when they returned, but their neighbors had only the burden of finding a *reasonably priced* tree service.

We were blessed that Matthew killed no one on Hilton Head.

We had no idea what to expect when meteorologists started predicting the island might get its first direct hurricane hit in a century. Our normal shrug-of-the-shoulders attitude about the threat changed on Tuesday, October 4, when then-South Carolina Governor Nikki Haley ordered the region to evacuate. That day the Category 4 storm hit Haiti and eventually killed 546 people.

Most people followed Gov. Haley's orders and fled west to Atlanta or north toward Charlotte, and places in between or beyond. A few hunkered down for the storm.

Matthew hit Florida at the end of the week, hugging the coast as it headed north. By Friday night, Hilton Head was in Matthew's sights. Down to a Category 2, its wind gusts peaking at 88 mph, the storm made its move onto the island the morning of October 8. The eye stayed between five and ten miles off the coast—just close enough to cause destructive flooding and roof-ripping, tree-toppling wind and tornadoes. Water, sewer and power were out for days in many areas, even after we were told we could return on October 11.

Some estimates say over 120,000 trees were downed on Hilton Head. County officials say that as of May 2017, almost 2.2 million cubic yards of vegetative debris had been gathered—enough to fill Madison Square Garden over five times.

When did we realize the extent of the tree destruction? Did it start with the incessant sound of tree grinding that breeched the normal quietness for months? Or did reality take a firmer hold when we started seeing water views and houses once hidden behind lush foliage? Perhaps it was when some golf courses finally reopened with wider fairways on holes once lined with trees.

The missing trees … when history finalizes the story of Hurricane Matthew and Hilton Head Island, it has to make note of the missing trees. Their loss is the one pain shared by all Hilton Head Islanders in the wake of Hurricane Matthew.

Epilogue: Eleven months after Matthew, on September 11, 2017, monster Hurricane Irma devastated the Caribbean and much of Florida before veering west, its far-flung outer bands doing damage hundreds of miles away from the eye. Hilton Head Island was lashed again, areas were flooded, but far fewer trees were lost. We were spared the worst. Humbled by nature, we know to batten down and evacuate. And hold dear our trees.

Sansing McPherson

Merry Debris

Elizabeth Robin

By Christmas, Hilton Head Island streets sport walls of immense pine logs. These line both sides of most streets, adorned randomly by stumps with gnarled roots, stacks of palmetto fronds, and branch after branch. The walls loom well over my head. I walk my dog carefully, now adept at navigating the narrowed way as cars and trucks approach. We duck into dents, safe enclaves among the detritus of Matthew. It will be months before back streets are cleared; it's worth the wait, as FEMA will cover seventy-five percent of the cost.

I spy a sliver of red ahead, wonder as I near it what sits atop this woodpile. I discern the form as I approach: Tall antlers from shredded bark, painted red. Centered sand dollars, also red. A bit of red ribbon. Large painted cartoon eyes. Twin Rudolphs emerge from the debris, and I find my Christmas card for 2016. I capture the image with my phone.

I know the house, the craft of the woman inside. She fashions jewelry out of found materials—shells, beads, wood, clay. I'm certain she decided to bedazzle her woodpile. *Bedazzle* is her favorite word. And the environs, post-Matthew, disturb artists more than most. It rattles their aesthetic sense. Artists not only represent their world, but amplify its beauty.

I appreciate immediately what she has done. Life dumped a pile of debris on her front lawn, but it does not dictate her mood. She alters the message. No longer destruction, trash, refuse from devastation, this pile props up—supplies, even—her Christmas decorations. Rudolph lives in that woodpile. Rudolph looks damn good up there.

I find more and more art installations as the months spool out after Matthew. Some mark the holidays, like those Rudolphs.

There had been October Jack O' Lanterns and Thanksgiving turkeys. Later snow flakes and hearts. One afternoon I spy the Van Gogh culprit crouched before one wood stack mid-spray. She casts a glance and a smile over her shoulder as I pass. She's become a graffiti elf, armed with spray cans and the imagination to recreate iconic art on the end of the heap of ten-foot pine segments placed at a random roadside corner. She fills this pile with her rendition of Starry Night, painted to scale. A museum installation to beautify the drive home.

By the time leprechauns are due, most of those woodpiles have cleared. My neighbor harvests as much wood as she can cut, carry and store, and gets busy. She makes angels and flowers, clever decor for gardens ravaged by both Matthew and the ensuing cleanup. Her new line of debris art sells out at the two local stores that carry it each time she replenishes inventory.

I can't help but see her art as the perfect metaphor for this year, as I learn how to be a widow. How do I reshape my life, after unbearable loss? Local artists show us: Take on that debris, and live artfully with it. Create beauty, even when life seems bleak. There are days it's a struggle, but there's a magnificence in how we learn to overcome our shared yet lonesome sorrows, and find joy in the life we are left.

I watched when my mother lost everything she owned in a warehouse fire and said, "We still have each other. That's what matters." And my father when he was widowed much too young, telling my brother and me what we'd do: "We'll go on."

The idea that we can take our debris and celebrate its potential, make it something beautiful, catches us. If we can turn tragedy into a newer, stronger self, we win. If my parents' lives expanded, then so can mine.

I relocated to Hilton Head Island from Point Pleasant Beach, New Jersey, two years before Superstorm Sandy roared through and devastated that town. But when friends' Facebook pages captured the aftermath, one picture stood out, reminding me of a similar moment ten days after I moved there in 1992, when another superstorm wreaked havoc two weeks before Christmas. In '92 I marveled as neighbors restrung their Christmas lights around the piles of their belongings heaped at the curb for pick-up. Entire contents ruined by ocean flooding, but lit for Santa.

And that 2012 Sandy photo? A house two doors down from mine, furnishings for the second time in twenty years piled out front. A white sheet, hung across the front of the house, spray-painted with red letters, our local school colors. It read: THE FEW. THE PROUD. THE BEACH. Banners like that draped the town for months in 1993, and again after Sandy. An in-your-face reminder of the tensile strength in survivors. I see so many people live this, and it inspires me each time.

Perhaps loss offers an opportunity, the chance once again to choose what we value, who we honor, how we live. We go on. Or we don't. It's a choice we make every day. Most islanders re-plant, reroof, restore this slice of paradise. Some relocate. Others review the statistics: How many times Madison Square Garden could be filled with our debris: Three times? Five? Ten? Downed tree estimates: 20,000? 50,000? 100,000? More? Obsess upon a future disastrous possibility and all the trees looming over them, absorbed by *next time*.

But somewhere, our lumber and mulch rebuilds a community, freshens its gardens. Somewhere, our story lifts others afraid to face a restart. And here, we embrace the creative energy of that life force called artists, enhancing our lives at their most dreary. Matthew— and those Rudolphs—gifted me, in my grief. A reminder I can go on with style. I can reconfigure life's debris into art.

VERTICALITY

Norm Levy

A tree stands
Tall
Upright
Lofty
Branches clawing skyward.
A silent sentinel
High above
The earth below.

And then
And THEN
AND THEN

Wind–flayed
Splintered
Twisted
Wrenched
Uprooted
Toppled
Fallen
Vertical no more.

What I see
Is no longer a tree.
What I see
Is debris

Matthew's Socks

~

Len Camarda

"Jeez," said Jennie, looking up at the kitchen television. "They don't know if it's gonna be a category one, two, or three hurricane, or if it will even make land."

"Doesn't matter," said Carl, Jennie's husband. "I've got us packed and ready to leave. I think we should get moving now, before traffic turns into a nightmare. We have a room reserved in Macon, so why not get started?"

"Let's wait. These things always pass us by."

"Well," Carl said, shrugging, "we're prepared either way. We have plenty of bottled water, the bathtub is full to the top and we have supplies of everything we need."

"And since the stove and barbeque are propane powered, no problem with food either," added Jennie, "but I still think it's gonna turn."

It was Wednesday, October 5, and the governor ordered mandatory evacuations for all areas east of I-95. It had started to rain on Hilton Head Island, and WTOC's weather team showed the hurricane coming toward Jacksonville, Florida. The projected paths of the storm had it going anywhere from making landfall around Jacksonville, veering out to sea, or going anywhere in between.

"Look," said Carl, "the traffic cams show light traffic all the way into Georgia. A good time to get on the road."

"Not yet," replied Jennie, looking down at their two toy poodles. "I know the dogs love to go for car rides, but this whole thing is going to be traumatic for Gina and Sophia. Better wait and take our chances with the traffic."

And so they waited. They kept WTOC around the clock and by Thursday, there was a steady rain, so Carl went out and lowered the level of the pool. By Friday the wind and the rain had picked up considerably. The hurricane had not hit, but they were in a real storm.

"We have to go. It looks real bad out there," urged Carl. "I checked with Macon, and all hotels are now booked up. We blew our reservation for Wednesday, but we can just keep driving toward Atlanta and call from the car 'til we find something?"

"Just keep driving all over the state with Gina and Sophia, hoping we find something?"

"They'll be fine. I'm going to check if the pool level is still down far enough, and then we're going," decided Carl.

Jennie kept staring at the television, looking defeated. Meanwhile, Carl went downstairs, put on some rain gear and ventured outside.

The level of the pool was up from all the rain, and he decided to take it down another foot or so. He had to leave the cover of the living room terrace above him to get to the pool service area. He was drenched in seconds by the time he made it to the shelter under the bedroom terrace. Then shock. Cowering there was a drenched little kitten.

"*What the hell...*" Carl said to himself. Bending down, he scooped up the kitten and brought it to his chest. "Where did you come from?" he asked the bedraggled little creature.

He still had to lower the pool level, so clutching the kitten in his left hand, he went out again into the storm. He opened the valve, then quickly ran back under the cover of the terrace. The kitten buried its head into Carl's shoulder as if it didn't want to see what was going on. Carl looked around, trying to imagine where this little creature came from and where its mother was. He checked the pool, found it low enough, ran back to close the valve and dashed into the garage with the kitten in his arm.

"Jennie, come here," he yelled up the stairs from the garage.

"What?" she answered. "Do we have a problem? Is water coming in?"

"No," he said as she came down the stairs. "Look what I found."

"Oh my God," gasped Jennie. "That poor thing. Where did you find it?"

"Under the bedroom terrace, just sitting there, shivering."

"Carl, you know if there's one kitten, there has to be more. And where is its mother? Can you look around for others?"

"You've got to be kidding," he protested.

"Please, Carl, just a quick look," she pleaded. "If it's bad, come back. I don't need you getting killed looking for kittens, but just a quick look. They have to be nearby. See if you can find the mother."

"Oh, man," muttered Carl, turning and going out the back door again. The rain was coming down almost sideways, and the wind was picking up. Venturing out was a challenge. Despite still being daytime, it was dark and gray, so Carl took a flashlight with him. He staggered toward the property line, thick with tall, whipping bamboo trees. He could barely see. He crouched down and began pushing the debris around the bamboo shrubs, shining the light back and forth. Nothing. He moved to the large azalea bushes and then to the side of the house, pausing around an extension ladder leaning there. He pointed the flashlight behind the ladder. He saw something. A face. A black face with a white spot on its forehead, half buried in pine straw. Another kitten. And next to it, a sister or brother. *Two more kittens. But where is Momma?*

Delicately retrieving the two little creatures from the pine straw, he looked around for others. Seeing none, he started back, still looking for Momma. A strong gust of wind drove Carl inside. He had to push hard to get the door closed against the wind. He kicked off his boots, shrugged out of his jacket and left everything on the garage floor in a wet heap, all the while cooing to the kittens. "No, no guys. It'll be okay. You're going to be okay," Carl said softly, bringing them to his face and snuggling them.

He went up to the kitchen, where Jennie was drying the first kitten.

"Now what do we do?" asked Carl, holding out #2 and #3.

"I thought there would be more of them," said Jennie. "Well, we're not driving anywhere now. Dry those guys off." She tossed Carl a towel. "Then dry yourself off. You look worse than they do."

Two girls and a boy. Mostly black, with a white patch on their chests and foreheads. And black legs with white paws. The girl Carl found first had two white front paws. The other girl had all four paws white, and the male had only one front white paw.

"You know," Jennie mused, "I remember seeing a black cat around here. It had one white paw and a small patch of white above its eyes."

"Yeah, I've seen it too. Think that's the mother?"

"Maybe," she shrugged. "The coloring is right. But where could she be? She wouldn't abandon her kittens unless something happened to her."

"More important, what's going on with the hurricane? I wanted to get out of here today," Carl said.

"Nothing definitive yet. Could come ashore, might move out to sea. They show half a dozen possible tracks. We're kinda in limbo."

"We're kinda in limbo with two dogs and three kittens," added Carl.

"They're probably only a couple of weeks old, the poor babies. We have to feed them. Give them some milk or something," said Jennie.

"That we can do," said Carl, handing Jennie a kitten. He moved to the refrigerator, holding another. "I'll warm some up to take the chill out of it. And look at Gina and Sophia," Carl remarked. "Just sitting there, looking at our new guests. Have they barked, or anything?"

"Nothing. Just sitting, looking at the kittens and then at each other. It's like they're thinking, "*Who are these guys?*""

Pouring the warmed milk into three saucers, Carl and Jennie put down their guests in front of the dishes. They picked up the dogs, just in case. All three felines went to the dishes and kind of played with the milk but didn't lap it up. "What's wrong with them? They don't like milk?" Jennie asked.

"I don't know, but I'm not sure milk is good for them anyway. While we can, we should make some calls or check the Internet on what to do."

"Okay," she said, "I'll do that. Then what?"

"We're here now for the duration. I suggest we eat something and then set up in the guest room for the night."

"Why the guest room?" she asked.

"The guest room has the second floor above it. If a branch comes crashing down, we're

protected in the guest room."

"Oh God, now you're scaring me. Maybe we should have left," Jennie lamented.

"But then we wouldn't have rescued these guys," Carl smiled. "They wouldn't have survived out there. What do you think we should call them?"

Jennie brightened. "What comes to mind is Socks, but we can't call all of them Socks."

"That's a good idea. What about One Sock, Two Socks and Four Socks," Carl said. "That will make it a lot easier to know who's who."

"A whole bunch of Socks. You're so clever," Jennie replied.

While Carl went to change into dry clothes, Jennie got the soft bed they used for the girls in the car. She put the kittens into the bed and covered them with a plush dishtowel, cautioning Gina and Sophia with a stern, "No," and then started to do some research.

Carl returned shortly, looking less wilted. "I see our Socks are sleeping. Did you find out anything?"

"No one answered at the Humane Association. I'll bet they evacuated with the rest of the island. Can you imagine trying to find safe shelter for all their dogs and cats? What a nightmare that had to be."

"I can't imagine," said Carl. "So, no information yet?"

"Oh, I found out quite a bit from the Internet, and we are in deep doo-doo."

"What do you mean?" asked Carl, his eyebrows knitting up.

"You were right. Cow's milk is not good for kittens. They talk about milk substitutes, but there's no way we will be able to get anything like that for a while. Evaporated milk might suffice. Plus two other goodies. Have to feed them by bottle, or something we can fashion for them to suckle on, and, get this, we have to stimulate their butts to poop."

"How do you stimulate their butts?" Carl asked incredulously.

Jennie sighed. "Well, apparently Momma cats lick the kitten's bottom to help them go to the bathroom. They just can't go on their own for several weeks."

"Well if I have to lick a kitten's bottom, they're going back outside," replied Carl.

"You're such an ass." Jennie smiled broadly.

"Don't say ass," said Carl. They both broke out in laughter.

"Look, we'll figure something out until we can talk to someone and get advice," he assured. "In the meantime, while they're snoozing, let's prepare something for us to eat and give our girls their dinner."

He fed the dogs while she prepared dinner. "Spaghetti with marinara sauce," Jennie announced. "While everything is still working, we'll get a good meal under our belts and then wait out the storm."

"And then figure out what and how to feed our little guests."

The spaghetti hit the spot, and while Jennie cleaned up, Carl went about figuring out how to feed the kittens. He found a can of evaporated milk and some grits in the pantry, and cooked them up to a loose mixture. Then he fashioned a bottle-like system using a plastic sandwich bag with a small hole in a corner. He filled the baggie and tried it out with One Sock. It worked. One Sock suckled the bag and took the concoction. Two Socks and Four Socks followed, and in a short time all had consumed their dinner.

"How soon after eating do you think they have to go to the bathroom?" Jennie asked.

"Well, if they are anything like Gina, it goes in and then it comes out. We'll wait a little while and then start the stimulation." He used a rubber glove with a smidge of Vaseline, and placed the kittens on the wee-wee pad they used for the dogs. Success! The kittens, one by one, piddled and indeed, made some deposits on the pad.

It was now close to evening, and Carl thought it was time to hunker down in the guest room. Fully dressed, they settled on each side of the bed with Gina and Sophia curling up beside them and the soft bed with all three kittens between them. The kittens snuggled up into what looked like one big fur ball and went to sleep. Jennie again covered them with the dishtowel. Television on, they kept up with Matthew while the animal menagerie slept. Occasional thumps on the roof from falling branches would awaken Sophia, ever vigilant, but in general the only thing they heard was the low roar of the wind. And there they stayed, into the night, watching and waiting.

They never slept, but the animals were lost in dreamland. Carl and Jennie would occasionally place their hand on the kittens to make sure they were breathing. Such soft and vulnerable little creatures, they seemed fine. Jennie and Carl would drift into the twilight zone every once in a while, but for the most part they remained glued to the television. Then, about 4:30 a.m., there was a blip, and everything went dark. Carl turned on his cell phone, went to WTOC's weather app, and continued to follow the storm on a smaller screen. Before long it began to brighten outside. The wind and rain had softened. The family had made it through the night and survived the perils of Matthew.

Carl went into the kitchen and turned on the portable radio. Matthew had moved past Hilton Head after almost a direct hit to the island. Things were improving. Then he looked out the window. The driveway was full of branches, some dangerously large. *What a mess!*

"How does it look?" asked Jennie.

"So far, not horrible. Lots of branches down, but the rain has just about stopped. I'll go out soon and check everything out."

"I can see the wind is still strong," said Jennie, looking out the guest room window, "so you're not going anywhere until things calm down."

Oddly enough, the morning started out as it usually did,

getting ready for the day; notwithstanding they had just been through a hurricane, had no electricity and had houseguests, who looked kind of frisky this morning. "I think these guys have recovered from their ordeal," Jennie remarked. "I'm not sure they're going to want to stay in that bed."

"We'll take it as it comes," said Carl. "Right now, a little coffee, maybe a lot of coffee, will be welcome."

He made coffee using an old percolator they had in the pantry. With the electricity still out, their plan was not to open the refrigerator unless it was absolutely necessary and the freezer not at all. Carl retrieved the kitten concoction he made last night and in a flash, shut the door. The dogs always went to their water bowl in the morning, and Carl thought he should give the kittens some water. He found a large squeeze dropper and used that to dispense water to the kittens. He thought he'd wait a while for the grits formula, hoping he would be able to reach somebody at the shelter first. When he called the Hilton Head Humane Association, miraculously, somebody picked up the phone.

"Oh God, am I glad to reach you," he said, and then proceeded to relate his story to one of the administrators, who had remained on the island. Most of the animals had been moved to Beaufort, but a few remained and had to be cared for, as there was no way to know when the island would be opened again.

She gave Carl a long list of things to do and not do. First, kittens so young do not usually survive without their mother, "So be prepared," she said. She had appropriate milk substitute at the shelter, but not knowing the conditions on the road, that option might not be open for a while. If Carl could get there, he'd be welcome to it. If not, he should add an egg yolk to the grits formula and hope for the best. She was alone at the shelter, so she thought the kittens would be better off where they were. She took Carl's phone number and said she would check with them periodically. If he found the roads were passable, he should come and get the substitute formula.

Carl got off the phone and found Two Socks at his feet. "Jennie, I think we have an escapee," he called out.

"Cripes, I just got One Sock corralled. I was straightening out the guest room, put their bed on the floor, and saw only Four Socks sitting there," she yelled back.

With everybody now in the kitchen, and Gina and Sophia looking totally confused, Carl said, "We still have that gate we used when the girls were puppies. I'll set the kittens up in the laundry room when we want to contain them. In the meantime, I need to feed them. The lady at the Humane Association said three times a day if they'll take it."

Carl and Jennie went through the day, eating things they could make on the stove, making calls to relatives and friends and chatting with the Humane Association from time to time. Jennie insisted Carl not go out yet because the wind could still bring branches down.

Sunday was different. The sun was out, the winds diminished. Time to get organized. First, clear the driveway in order to get the cars out, recharge the cell phones from the cars, and if the roads were clear, get to the Humane Association. Carl worked all morning sawing branches into manageable pieces and moving them to the front side of the driveway. Looking down the street, he saw he would be going nowhere until some really big branches were moved; they were too big for him to handle.

Then, another shock. At the corner of his property sat a black cat with a white patch on its face, and beside it, a kitten with what looked like three white paws, staring at him. The mother and another sibling. *How did they survive?*

Carl ran into the house. "Jennie, Jennie," he called, "the mother is here! Can you believe it? Call the shelter! What do we do now?" He went back outside to keep track of the mother cat and the kitten with her, speculating that maybe that kitten had strayed from the nest, Momma went to get it, and the fury of the storm hit, separating them from the rest of the family.

Jennie was back in a few minutes. "She said the best thing is to reunite the kittens with their mother. It's best for them."

"That's it? Just stick them outside again and let nature take its course? Look, stay there and keep an eye on Momma. I want to talk to them."

Carl came back out shortly, looking dejected. "Yeah, that's it. She said to put them back where we first found them. We can put the bed they've been using there, and we can put food out for the mother every day. She'll need it. I'll put a water bowl out there also. In a couple of weeks, when they're weaned, the shelter would like to come out. Hopefully catch the mother, have her spayed and collect the kittens for adoption."

They cleaned storm litter from the space where Carl found the kittens and put canned tuna out until they got to the store and bought cat food. The kittens always came around when Carl or Jennie visited, and even Gina and Sophia would drop by and frolic with them. Momma's milk seemed to be working well. Carl and Jennie also made a decision. They would adopt Two Socks, the kitten that started this whole thing. A friend wanted Four Socks, and they were sure the other two would be placed quickly by the shelter after Momma got fixed.

Cats have nine lives. With Momma and all the Socks, that's forty-five lives together. They needed some of those to get through Matthew, perhaps conveying a few of them to Jennie and Carl.

The Second Hurricane

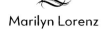

Marilyn Lorenz

Fran was my first hurricane. She hit the family room in our house in Raleigh in the middle of the night, hurling two dogwood trees and a rather substantial pine through new gutters and freshly painted doors, effectively preventing escape if I had been inclined to try. But I was sitting on the floor of the downstairs powder room wrapped in the paws of an overprotective West Highland White Terrier, terrified.

Fran tossed twelve pieces of iron balcony furniture through the deck railing and into the woods three hundred yards away. She raged more than four hours, screeching and tearing up the neighborhood in an out-of-control rampage. We were asleep in the powder room before dawn, curled together afraid to open our eyes. But wake we did, to chaos everywhere. It took a month to repair Fran's wrath, and I don't remember it fondly. So, when the National Weather Service and the local weather channels began predicting Matthew's path toward our new home on Hilton Head Island, we packed and left without a moment's hesitation, loaded to the gills with irreplaceable items and our overexcited cockapoo, Bogey. I wasn't sticking around for a second encounter with Mother Nature at her worst.

Lucky for us, the retirement community where we were living had made reservations well in advance at the Aloft Ballantyne in Charlotte. So off we went, sure of our destination and feeling confidently ahead of whatever Matthew held in store. Of course everyone else of a cautionary nature was already on the road, nervously nibbling their supply of snacks and subject to fits of pique at the slightest alteration in traffic pattern. We crawled, substantially under the speed limit, for miles and miles. Bogey sat up in his crate, all twenty-five pounds of curly cockapoo exuberance on high alert, excitedly wagging and barking at all the other dogs on the road. Unfortunately all the other dogs did the same thing, accompanied by meowing cats, creating a cacophony heard through shushing humans and rolled up windows. I hate to think of the amount of pollution from idling SUVs and shuddering vans that pumped into local air before we were able to split off from the maddening crowd and head toward Charlotte. But what the heck, Matthew was coming, and Matthew would do more than clean our air.

Four hectic driving hours later, the Ballantyne area of Charlotte became an arrow on the global positioning system in our car, and before long found our beautiful hotel. We were surprised and delighted, having never experienced real luxury in a pet friendly hotel. It was new and sleek, glass and stainless steel, cheerfully providing every sparkling amenity throughout every room. We were quickly ensconced and set off on a walking tour to discover the neighborhood before dark.

The Ballantyne golf course, directly behind our hotel, was tucked in the last rays of a beautiful October sunset as we set off down the path to stretch our legs. It must have been a busy day on that course because Bogey's nose plowed through grass and rough as if something precious were just ahead. In waning light we trotted down three golf holes before returning to the comfort of our room. Armed with potato chips, drinks, sandwiches and dog food, we settled down, watching Mathew's unfolding drama on our big screen TV. No doubt everyone in the hotel was similarly occupied. Matthew was the news, the story, the stark fear of the day. But in this hotel, we were safe.

Most of the weather channels were listing Matthew as a Category 3 hurricane, and they began endlessly replaying every horrifying film clip they could find. The breaking waves along the coast, the water flowing down streets and inland byways, the soaked weathermen falling backwards clutching caps and umbrellas, miraculously continuing to deliver the news through gale force winds and pelting debris. It was like we were watching a movie, and it seemed far away. None of it looked real. When we couldn't stand watching anymore, we took Bogey out for a last piddle and tucked in for the night. The worst was yet to come, and we figured it would all play out with or without us watching.

Well, it did play out before daybreak, and every channel on television carried video after video of falling trees, flailing branches, exhausted weather people and water overwhelming everything in its path. We were eating breakfast in front of the television when a clip came on covering the hurricane and tornadoes on Hilton Head Island. It was painful to see how much damage there was, how extensively Matthew had changed the landscape of our beloved island. We cried, knowing so much we had taken for granted would never be the same again. Then we began to plan the journey home.

On Saturday morning Hilton Head Island was closed to all but emergency vehicles. State officials had ordered guards to monitor every approach, checking licenses, addresses, and effectively denying access. The reasons given were eminently reasonable.

No power, precarious conditions, high standing water, and impassable roads. All the facts you would expect, and some that no one expected. So we bought more sandwiches, potato chips and beer, walked Bogey between raindrops, and continued watching the saga unfold on TV. By now Bogey was in continuous party mode, because downstairs in the lobby were friends! The minute he got in the elevator, his tail would wag so fast we thought it was sure to fall off. It was hard to hold him when the elevator doors opened and there were all his buddies, barking and sniffing and delighted to see him!

Frankly, all the dogs partying made it more than a little challenging. Every human was showing signs of stress. People rushed from elevator to barstool shouting into their cell phones, as dogs tangled leashes in an absolute frenzy of happiness. The bar area, crowded to the gills with creatures seeking solace, pulsed apprehensively into the wee hours of Sunday morning. By dawn, according to the governor of South Carolina, we were still in a state of emergency, and no one would be allowed back on Hilton Head Island. So Sunday strung out like bubblegum, snapping, popping and getting old. I'm telling you, nothing is worse than not being able to get home when you're apprehensive about what you're going to find when you get there.

Monday found us all tense, short tempered, and leaving our dogs (except when necessary) in our rooms, in spite of hotel regulations to the contrary. The bar area was the meeting place for everyone, and we eagerly shared whatever news we could. Some crazy person had walked onto the island at night, slept on a porch, and taken pictures on their cell phone of every neighborhood they could access. The pictures weren't pretty, but they made the rounds quickly from hand to hand, bearing clear, stark evidence of Matthew's passing. Tuesday at 8 a.m. we checked out and headed south, not a bit sure of how far we would be able to drive.

I have to say, Governor Haley and the South Carolina Department of Transportation communicated regularly on all the stations on the car radio. We were updated on conditions in a factual, professional manner almost every hour of our trip. It was a grim scene when we arrived in the Lowcountry, because just the most crucial cleanup of major highways had started. Only emergency vehicles were being allowed across the bridge to Hilton Head Island. Luckily for us, one of our daughters had just been allowed back into her home in Moss Creek, just off island. She enthusiastically invited us to stay with her, explaining that she needed all the help she could get. With trepidation, we pulled into Moss Creek and made our way around felled trees, roof shingles, blown detritus of gigantic proportions, and standing water. Kim's home stood miraculously untouched amid downed trees you couldn't reach around. It seemed like the only thing unbroken by Matthew was the house and garage, and even they were covered in snapped branches, uprooted plants, far flung bird houses, and sad remnants. There wasn't a single square inch of undisturbed yard. A literal ton of work lay ahead to even begin to see the ground. So we set to it, the three of us, glad that at least the power was on in Moss Creek, so we could continue to work after nightfall. We heated up old frozen pizza, drank a few beers, and slept like marathon runners after a race.

Wednesday, Thursday and Friday we picked up storm debris and carried it to the curbs in Moss Creek. That is all we did, sunup to sundown, every single day. Hilton Head was declared "unsafe" due to contaminated water, dangerous road conditions, hanging tree limbs, and no power supply except for emergency generators. Thanks to incessant cell phone activity among neighbors and friends, word began to filter through the grapevine about the worst hit neighborhoods, the highest standing water, the docks that had floated away, and the boats that were missing. We worked at Kim's until Saturday morning, when ordinary residents of Hilton Head, like us, were finally cleared to return.

Crossing the bridge to the island was an otherworldly experience. All we could do was stare at the damage, and pray silently that our property had been spared the worst of it. At the back gate to Hilton Head Plantation, a hand painted sign leaned precariously against a great ball of dirty roots, wobbling a shaky "Welcome Home." Bogey, sensing something awry, sat quietly in his crate. We kept going, noting mounds of destruction twenty feet high in some places, lining forests and fields, lagoons and pathways. Then, after what seemed like an eternity, we were home.

Miraculously, we could find no sign of Matthew anywhere. All the windows were intact. No sign of water seepage on rugs or around doors. No roof damage immediately apparent. So the fact that the golf course was torn up, that trees and branches had toppled every which way, that bushes and plants were scattered as far as the eye could see, didn't seem important. Across the road, our friends and neighbors were telling a different story. Massive tree trunks had cut through living rooms and doorways, family rooms and kitchens. Soaked rugs lined driveways, ruined beyond repair. Screaming buzz saws and front loaders plowing debris into huge dump trucks caught the afternoon sun, and the backbreaking, heartbreaking, labor of recovery began.

Gradually, birds and critters returned to new habitats and new homes, and the island human population strained ahead under the weight of loss and change. Every day, a little more foliage and a few more trees left the island, piled high in out-of-state dump trucks. Every day the holes in our forests widened and deepened, making clearings where there were none, opening space we had never seen. And in that space were the things that made us saddest of all. Our native island population, the Gullah people, living here since before the Civil War, had been hit very hard. Old shacks sheltering the working poor, had in many cases, not fared well. The lesson of Matthew, in stark contrast to the recovery we witnessed in the more affluent plantations and neighborhoods, was that our working poor were suffering Matthew's wrath in ways we had not had to consider. For them it would be a long, long recovery, if indeed recovery came at all. And yet, as always, they were out laboring on behalf of those able to pay them, restoring order to chaos so that others might enjoy their former lives with a minimum of inconvenience.

There is a fury to my sadness these days. I am urging consciences wherever I go to pay attention, to follow through on promises made to the poor in the wake of Matthew's passing. We needed them. They need us now. Time to step up.

The Windsurfer

Terri L. Weiss

January

My pink-and-green batik print tunic flutters against me in the ocean wind. Wearing anything but solid black or quiet neutrals runs counter to my origins. I paid full price, too, albeit inadvertently—nothing any self-respecting New Yorker would do. I didn't even flinch when I signed *Mira Sinclair* on the credit card screen. Eighteen hundred miles justifies whatever I do here. That, along with my still quasi-intact severance pay and landing a job in a Sea Pines design store, has me in an island state of mind.

From my position on the dune ramp, five—no, six—windsurfers skim across the water, an array of red and blue sails billowing above their black wetsuits. It's January, and although island temperatures have soared into the low seventies, I bet the water is frigid.

I cup one hand above my sunglasses to form a makeshift visor. Curls of water at least two feet high crest, then swoop onto the sand. That unmistakable *hooooh* fills my ears.

One of the windsurfers topples into the water, and two more follow. The wind carries the laughter of those still gliding above the waves, until something causes them to capsize. In a flash, all six are atop their boards once more. Coming to shore to land, I suspect.

With the sun this bright, it would be pointless to check my iPhone for the time, but the heat on my skin tells me I've been out too long. My skin is so pale it never bronzes, instead turning a ruddy shade that feels as angry as it looks.

An extra minute won't matter. I pack my beach duffel, one item at a time, rather than in my usual toss-it-all-in-who-cares style. But when I glance at the ocean again, the windsurfers have vanished. How foolish to have risked sun damage because of two-decade-old memories of good-looking beach bums and far riskier holiday breaks. I turn my back to the water and head up the ramp, toward the trails.

And that's when I spot them again: A group of lycra-clad men in the parking lot, packing windsurfing equipment onto pickups. All have gray hair, and all but one have paunches. The flat-bellied man is taller and broader than the rest, and has a long ponytail. He turns to me and winks, then hops in his truck and drives away.

★★★

February

Scores of cats lounge in the sun along both sides of the roadway to the Hilton Head Humane Association. I've slowed to five miles an hour in case one bolts across the asphalt, but the cats don't budge at the sound of my car. Like bears in national parks, I suppose, unfazed by humans as long as we don't approach on foot.

As I ease into the closest available parking space, a black pickup zooms into the striped zone in front of a "No Parking" sign. The engine cuts, and the driver jumps out and thwacks his door shut with an authoritative thud. I swear under my breath: *People like that think they own the world.*

I'm still fussing in my car, when Genghis Khan disappears into the office. He charges back outside, an empty dog lead dangling from his hand. One of the volunteers trots behind him, dropping further back every second. I curse under my breath again—how oblivious can this guy be?

I refuse to let him spoil my mood, not in a place abounding with cats. Although I've completed an adoption application for a tabby named Buddy, I might take one or two more home. After all, my son's away in college, my ex-husband's in Maine; I can do what I want. So I head up the path toward the office.

A sharp bark makes me turn around. Genghis Khan has hooked up the lead to a large dog that is leaping all over him. Then he laughs, and kneels on the ground to hug his new rescue pup. Belly rubs follow.

Honestly, I could kick myself for making assumptions.

At that moment, the man pivots and looks straight at me. That's when I notice his long gray ponytail.

"I absolutely love adoption days," says a voice behind me. "Are you Mira?"

"Yes." I linger until the man returns to his pickup, accompanied by his canine companion. He opens the front door, and the dog leaps inside.

I'm not sure, but I think he just waved goodbye. To me.

★★★

March

Madeline, one of my tennis partners, flips the pages of her program, and thrusts it at me. "I am so totally not into this. How long until intermission?"

The symphony is tuning from an oboe's A, and the resulting cacophony of woodwinds, strings and brass sends shivers down my spine. "Best sound ever," I whisper.

The featured pianist tonight is last year's winner of the International Piano Competition. Sixteen years old, for heaven's sake, and from a YouTube clip I'd heard, he promises to be more than your basic virtuoso; he promises to be lyrical. To bring tears to my eyes. To strike me in the soul with every chord he plays.

I push my hair from my face. Only a few minutes remain until they start.

Madeline nudges my elbow. "Will they have a bar set up, or just soft drinks?"

"Dunno, don't care." I settle into the pew, and start to read the pianist's bio. "You wanted to dress up, so stop complaining."

Madeline gleams with gold and pearls, and whether they're real or not is irrelevant. Jewelry is everywhere tonight, not the usual Hilton Head scene at all. The walls and ceilings glint from the reflection of halogens on a sea of gold and silver. Even I have some bling on—not for full price, of course.

Applause erupts as the conductor, in a black tuxedo only

slightly darker than his hair, marches into the hall. He nods at the audience, then picks up a mic to introduce the baby-faced piano prodigy, also donned in a tux. As the conductor mounts the podium and poises his baton over the music, the prodigy assumes his position behind a Steinway grand, and adjusts the piano bench. A few tugs on his cuffs, and he's all set.

The conductor's eyes scan the musicians arrayed before him. Up goes his baton ... and *down*. Immediately, the concerto's "announcement" fills the hall: The opening E-flat major chord of the full orchestra, to which the prodigy responds immediately with a credenza of sixteenth and thirty-second notes that cascade and trill, up and down the keyboard until the next grand symphonic chord.

Beethoven's Fifth Piano Concerto, first time I've ever heard it live.

When the main theme of the allegro begins, I lean forward to catch every note, every pause, every crescendo and decrescendo. My eyes well up, my heart quickens.

We are in the third row from the front, on the right side of the stage. Directly behind the two rows of double basses. One of the bass players has a long gray ponytail. Heat rushes into my face. Because of the music, I tell myself.

★★★

April

Every morning for the past two weeks, I've gone to the beach. I've moved all appointments to the afternoon and evening, I've missed six days of tennis. The island's southernmost beaches, where I first saw my windsurfer—he's become *mine* since the symphony—have been bereft of rigs ever since. I've hung out at Coligny, North Forest, even Folly Field, all to no avail. I'm beginning to feel like a wannabe groupie, *sans* binoculars, how embarrassing is that for a woman in her mid-forties? Each time, I tell myself: This is the last morning I'll waste, especially when they want to increase my hours at the store.

Seriously, it's today or bust. I bike to the Sea Pines Beach Club, lock up the bike in a rack, and hoist my bag over my shoulder. Gray clouds hint at rain, and, as I head toward the water, regret overcomes the last vestiges of curiosity about my windsurfing, dog-rescuing, bass-playing non-acquaintance.

I lean against a railing of the dune ramp. After a minute of peering toward the ocean, several black dots appear on the horizon. Windsurfing sails, I'm sure of it. They grow larger and larger by the moment. My heartbeat fills my eardrums as every wave brings them closer toward the beach where I'm standing. As the sails drop to the water a few dozen yards out, the windsurfers crouch on their boards. They're ashore now, disconnecting the rigs.

I think I spot a gray ponytailed man among those tugging equipment across the sand. I hope I'm wrong; otherwise, what would I say or do if he approached me? My mouth goes dry. When one of the windsurfers calls to the others, I force my legs to move as if wearing cement boots. Right foot, left foot, up and over the ramp toward the Beach Club.

At last I'm at the café, and plop onto a corner seat. Plenty of time to get my act together, and check my texts as if that's all I came here to do.

"Can I get you something?" The voice is male, the accent slightly European.

I look up, expecting to see a name-tagged server, likely a seasonal guy from the Southern Hemisphere.

But it's him. His shadow swallows the sun. I hadn't realized he was so tall.

"Saw you at the shelter, saw you at the symphony. And on the beach." He grins. "You following me, or maybe the other way around?"

I'm generally more articulate beyond saying "uhhhh."

He tugs over a seat and sits opposite me. His hair is loose and wet. "Grayson Hayward."

I reach for my bag. "I have a towel."

He crinkles his eyes, and his smile widens, revealing perfect teeth. "I'd rather have your name."

Before I can answer, the server appears, donning a tag: Kelvin. "Nice to see you again today, Ms. Sinclair. Island tea, or something else?"

Grayson answers for me, "Whatever Ms. Sinclair wants, make it two."

His eyes, slightly less crinkled now, are almost totally black, as if there are no irises. Like looking into infinity...

The server clears his throat. "Do you need a minute to decide, ma'am?"

"Island tea, thanks, Kelvin." After he scurries off, I draw a quick breath. The lines on Grayson's face give him at least ten years on me, but anyone would kill for that muscle definition.

"Still waiting on your first name," Grayson says.

"I'm Mira. And yes, of course, I'm following you." I laugh, as if I'm joking.

"How long are you here?" he asks. The standard question on this resort island.

"Permanently." I don't wear a wedding ring, not anymore, but I glance pointedly at the golden bamboo ring swirled around my left fourth finger. After all, I'm not that available and I'm not that easy.

"I'm on Daufuskie," he answers. "Year round."

"Why there?" I ask, as if it's any of my business that he lives on a tiny island, accessible only via boat.

"Don't like too many people around, unless they're on the water or playing music with me. Or listening, the way you did the other night."

"I have a thing for the Emperor Concerto." I'm reluctant to reveal more to a professional musician.

"The Emperor Concerto might have a thing for you, too, Mira."

I groan. "Omigod, try that on somebody else." My tone rises, and so do I.

Grayson stands also. "Please don't go." He extends his right hand. "Please?"

I wait, then accept his hand. His grip is warm, but not overly dominant like one of those crusher-grips. I have to admit, my hand feels right in his. Too right.

"Suppose I meant it, which I did?" he asks. "Would that matter?" He's still holding my hand.

"No."

Here come our drinks; I'd almost forgotten about them. I give Kelvin, the server, a half-smile, and free my hand. Then sit and motion to Grayson to do the same. I'm not about to skunk Kelvin—never mind Grayson, no matter how annoyed I am.

"Thanks for not running off on me." Grayson takes both our drinks from the tray, and hands me one. With his thumb, he wipes the frost from his glass. When it reappears, he repeats the attempt. Then he tries to adjust the drink menu, encased in plastic, in the center of the table, but it flops over. When he reaches to pick it up, his elbow sends his spoon clattering onto the floor.

I swallow a grin: *This guy is the farthest thing from smooth.*

"You play anything? Music, I mean?" he asks, after draining half his glass.

"I can feel it." When I was a conservatory student, those powered by ambition and discipline locked themselves away in practice rooms, day and night. Me, on the other hand...

"Feeling it is all that matters." Another swig, then he adds, "Must be pretty obvious that I generally don't sit down with women I don't know."

"Hope that's not another line," I say.

Grayson studies my face before speaking again. "Bosco," he says finally. "He's part chocolate lab, part Newfoundland, at least that's what they told me at the shelter."

"I adopted two gray tabbies that day. Denali and Puck."

"Great names." Grayson flags down the server. "I'll take the check."

"Wait a second." Reaching over, I touch his forearm, feeling veins under the tattoos. "Divorced, former New Yorker. A son in college. Excessively rude and defensive, love animals, hate lies."

"Twice widowed, originally from Copenhagen, don't expect

life to treat me right. No kids, no addictions except music. And I don't lie." He covers my hand with his again. "Nice to meet you."

★★★

October

Warmth seeps into my belly. I'm a glutton when it comes to cheddar cheese and tomato omelets, the best breakfast on the planet. Last night was Grayson's turn to come over, which means my condo smells great.

Over the past six months, Grayson has demonstrated that he is a true master of culinary arts, and I've demonstrated how easy it is for me to gain ten pounds. At five foot three, I can't afford to put on that much, but so far, Grayson hasn't commented. Even though he's inspected every last inch of me, from head to toe.

I've done the same to him, of course, and have found no flaws, save a few scars that make him even sexier than I'd ever imagined after those first heady weeks in April. Then, as now, we haven't spent more than a few hours apart from each other: He gets his music and rig time; I get my tennis and writing time. Work has grown more hectic, following my promotion to assistant manager; symphony season is in full swing for Grayson. None of that interferes with what we have, though.

Someday we'll get sick of each other, maybe even break up, but this moment—really, all these moments and hours and days, and especially nights? I swear, Grayson and I have breathed new meaning into Einstein's theory of relativity.

"Wind's starting to pick up." He scrubs the skillet while he talks. "They say this'll be the big one."

Bosco, curled into a semicircle, licks his paws. Grayson never goes anywhere without him, except to the symphony.

"Storms always miss the island, I'm not worried." I rub Bosco's head, then join Grayson at the sink to wipe down the dishes.

"Got to head home and tie everything down, just in case."

Both of us spin around at the clamor of toenails against the floor.

"Bosco, don't chase the cats." Grayson's tone is mild, and the dog races out of the kitchen anyway. Two blurs of tabby fur fly into the bedroom.

"Don't go." I drop the dishes in the sink and pull him toward me. His lips are soft on mine. "The ocean's really rough."

He pulls a sweatshirt over his head and leans over for another kiss. "Don't worry, Mira, I'll be back this afternoon. No rehearsal tonight, remember?"

I continue at the sink, hearing the gravel crunch under the tires of his truck. Bosco runs back into the kitchen and howls. One of my kitties must have tried to teach him a lesson.

★★★

It's dinnertime and Grayson hasn't returned my calls. The governor has issued an order to evacuate the island. I don't want to go, not without Grayson. The dog is huddled under the bed, and I find the cats underneath a pile of sweaters in the closet.

My neighbor, a volunteer firefighter with Grayson's former unit, knocks on my door for the third time today. "Mira, you have to leave."

"Tide's rising and I'm not leaving without him."

"He'll be okay," he says, patting my shoulder. "Probably just out of battery power."

"I don't know that, and you don't know that either." My voice rises.

Would Grayson please return one of my calls? Even emergency workers and first responders are evacuating. Everyone, except, from what I hear, a few crazies. Grayson must be among them.

A garbage can careens down the street.

"Get your animals together, time to stop being noble. Grayson's a big boy." My neighbor spots the dog lead. "Get the cats, get the dog, let's get you out of here. Unless you want to scare the bejesus out of them."

I find Bosco in the closet—the same one the cats are in—flattened against the floor. If I force these guys to stay through the storm, with the rain pounding down and wind ripping around the house, they could be traumatized for life. Hooking the lead on Bosco's collar, I tug him out of the closet. My neighbor shoves the cats, along with the sweaters they're hiding under, into the carriers, and helps me get them into my car. The dog cowers on the back floor.

As I pull away from the house, I wonder what it will look like when I return. For the millionth time, I tap the speed dial. Grayson's phone rings ten times, then goes to voice mail.

★★★

Five endless days pass before the authorities let us return to the island. Still no word from Grayson, and now his phone goes straight to voice mail, so I know his batteries are dead.

I startle at the familiar chime of my cell phone.

"Mira?" It's Ivan, one of Grayson's windsurfing buddies. "They found something."

"Where's Grayson?" I answer. "I've been going out of my mind."

Silence fills my ears.

"His rig. They found it. Mast's broken, sail's ripped up, but the board's in one piece."

"Where … is … Grayson?" I'm shouting and I don't care.

"That's all there is." More silence. "I'll contact you if they find anything else."

"What about his house? Did they check it? And his truck?" My pitch is three octaves higher than usual and my voice is shaking. "Have they checked the hospitals? Have they posted signs? Maybe someone found him injured and decided to take him in. Who's in charge, anyway?"

"Everything's gone, Mira. The house, his vehicle, totally destroyed by the storm. They say a bunch of tornados touched down …"

"Where is Grayson? He could be in a coma somewhere, or have amnesia."

"No one knows, Mira, sorry. I'll call if I hear anything further."

***

The Following April

The New Year has come and gone. The next piano competition, also come and gone. A new bass player occupies Grayson's place in the symphony.

As the sun sets on another April evening, Bosco and I head out to the beach. He sits in the sand facing the ocean. The authorities continue to say that no one died in South Carolina from the hurricane last fall, and I believe them. I've shared that with Bosco, whose tail wags in agreement each time I remind him. I'm willing to guarantee he understands English.

I shake out my beach towel in the wind and let it fall to the sand in a rumpled heap. I plop down next to Bosco, more off the towel than on, and kick away my flip flops. Burying my toes in the sand, I face the ocean, too. Then I throw my arms around Bosco, and touch my forehead right behind his ear, where his fur is softer than down. If I close my eyes tight enough, I can smell Grayson in the salt wind.

A boat horn moans across Calibogue Sound. A low F, Grayson always said. He had perfect pitch. Regardless, I used to say it was as deep and unflinching as the water deep below.

The boat sounds a low F again, but this time, it's followed by a staccato blast of whistles.

Grayson's coming back soon. I can feel it.

Kendra Natter

Morning After Matthew

Marilyn Lorenz

Lost leaves settle in slit tree trunks,
shrouding every path.
Unearthed roots on dying trees
tangle hopelessly together.

Abandoned homes fold their shattered frames
in a nightmare of swirling water,
the tortured ghosts for whom
there is no escape.

Picking breakfast of soggy detritus,
flitting nervously crumb to crumb,
a Cardinal survives the confusion,
of waking spared.

He searches endlessly the piled debris,
back and forth over severed branches,
hovering stunned and silent,
looking for home.

Cynthia Van Nus

Memories Lost and Found

Will Anderson

Jeanne Davis finished the employee schedules for the next week, posted them online, and turned off her computer. It was nearly 8:00 p.m. As the hotel's operations supervisor, she often worked late. Single, living alone without pets, working late was not a problem, even on a Friday. She put on a sweater, ignored the work-filled briefcase staring up from the desk top—*it will still be there on Monday*—and left her office. She locked the door, entered the hotel's main hall, and headed for the garage.

The hall took her past the front desk. The sound of high heels striking the floor caught the attention of two male clerks. As she walked past, their eyes followed the tall attractive woman with dark brown hair, a tiny waist and narrow hips. They smiled. She smiled back. *Acquaintances. Nothing more.*

Her route took her by the main restaurant. Beside the open door, the staff had hung a large menu. One item caught her attention, Surf and Turf—rib eye steak, seasoned, grilled, and topped with a choice of sea scallops or large gulf shrimp. *M-m-m.*

With little in the fridge at her condo, the promise of pleasing flavors, and the aroma emanating from the restaurant, deliberation took only a moment. She entered; the maître d quickly by her side. They chatted as he took her to a table by a window, held the chair while she sat down, and handed her a menu. The window overlooked the hotel pool, the beach, and the ocean beyond. *Best seat in the restaurant.* A waitress arrived a moment later. Jeanne asked for a glass of chardonnay and ordered the Surf and Turf.

As was her habit, she looked at the patrons, table by table, playing a game guessing who they were, what they did, and what they were talking about. She stopped when the wine arrived, took a sip and looked out at the beach and the ocean. Hilton Head Island. *No better place on Earth. Not for me.*

And then he walked in! Paul Hansen.

★★★

Jeanne had met Paul three months earlier on the Tuesday the South Carolina governor ordered the evacuation of the state's coastal areas as Hurricane Matthew, the tenth worst hurricane in U.S. history, approached. The hotel had closed that afternoon. They were both taking a last walk on the beach before leaving, she to her condo, he to his home in Virginia. Conversation ensued about the coming hurricane, the evacuation order, the hotel closing, his ruined vacation.

Casual rapport became friendly, then more than friendly. She found him attractive, easy going, and witty. She invited him to her condo for dinner. That evening, after the dinner, the wine, and the after-dinner wine, he accepted an invitation to spend the night. They enjoyed all that naturally followed. And with cell phone alerts telling them that Matthew would curve out to the sea, they spent two more days and nights together on the island.

But on Friday morning, they had heard a new forecast: Matthew would arrive on Saturday, its eye passing just offshore. Matthew would deliver 100 mile-per-hour winds, heavy rain, and cause extensive flooding. Jeanne and Paul decided to leave. They would take his Range Rover—safer in the wind and rain than her small Prius. The Range Rover was parked in the building complex's visitor lot, a one-minute walk from the condo. After both had packed, he took his suitcase and went out to get the vehicle. She watched him through a front window as he hurried away, fighting the wind, until he disappeared behind a row of trees that hid the lot from her view.

Anticipating his quick return, she had put her two suitcases just inside the front door, donned a raincoat, and gone to the front window expecting to see him drive up. But after several minutes seeing no sign of him, she grew worried and called his cell phone. When he didn't answer, she left a message telling him to call back as soon as he could.

Determined to learn what had happened, she decided to check out the visitor's lot. With the wind howling and heavy rain pouring down, she made her way to the lot and around the row of trees. One, she noticed, had been knocked over by the wind, some of its branches lying about the lot. She stared at each of the few parked vehicles but saw no Land Rover. *Where is it? And where is Paul?*

With dire feelings, she had spent minutes looking in parking places of nearby building lots, mostly empty, but did not spot the Rover or any sign of Paul. Not wanting to get her phone wet, she waited until back in the condo to call the neighbors she knew to ask if they had seen the Rover or a man walking outside. None of those that answered were still in the complex, however. They had left to avoid the hurricane. *Why didn't we leave ... couple of idiots!*

She had dialed 911 and explained the situation. The response was polite but not helpful. They repeated what seemed so obvious. Paul had gone to the Rover and driven away. They implied that she was in a much better position then they were to guess why. And in the context of an approaching hurricane, with the dozens of situations they were already handling, and with no known personal injury or damaged property, there was nothing they could do. After the call, she felt like smashing the phone against a wall but managed to calm herself.

She had stayed in the condo as the storm arrived, alternating between fear for her safety and concern for Paul. The storm did its harm, and moved on. Her building received minor damage, her condo none. After several still unhelpful calls to various authorities, and more to Paul's phone hearing the same message, she stopped making the calls. Like the storm, Paul had arrived, been a great partner for three days, but then moved on. Now it was her turn to move on. She put both experiences in a mental jar, put a lid on the jar, and put the jar on the very back of a seldom used shelf in her brain.

★★★

Jeanne snapped back to the present, staring wide-eyed as he was seated, handed a menu, and perused it. When he looked up, she still stared. He turned toward her, tilted his head, narrowed his eyes, and gave her a puzzled look. She returned the look with intensity. He rose and walked to her table. Tall, broad shouldered, handsome …

"Excuse me," he said. "I don't mean to be rude but I saw you staring and … this is an odd question, I admit, but … do you know me?"

Still staring directly at him, she took a deep breath, and after a moment of silence, answered curtly, "that's not funny."

"So you do know me?"

"For three days, I thought I did."

"Forgive me, and I truly mean that," he said. "But I suffered a head injury about three months ago and have no memories for a week or so before it happened. The doctors called it a form of retrograde amnesia."

"You don't remember getting the injury?"

"No. Nor anything for the prior week."

Her eyes narrowed. "You're telling the truth, not stringing me along … right?"

"You don't make up what I've been through."

She gestured he sit at her table. "Tell me what happened."

He took the offered seat. "Something must have hit me on the head. A flying branch I think."

She remembered the fallen tree and the branches.

"My brain bounced around. Bruises. A tear. Then bleeding through the tear that raised the pressure inside my skull and caused more damage. Enough to wipe out a week's worth of memories and bring on a host of other problems."

"Do you know where it happened?"

"In a parking lot not far from here."

That rings true. "Did it knock you out?"

"I don't know," he said, slowly shaking his head. "What I remember is finding myself on the ground, managing to get to my feet, looking around, and having no idea where I was or what I was doing there."

"What did you do then?"

"Looked for my phone. Spotted it under a large branch, smashed and unusable. Had my car keys though. Pushed the lock button on the fob and heard a beep."

"Range Rover."

"You do know me," he said, a smile forming.

"Did know you … three days worth."

A frown replaced his smile. "Not a good three days."

She smiled. "Actually a great three days … until it ended." The smile faded.

The waitress arrived and placed her entrée before her. The aroma promised great flavor.

"I'll have the same," he told the waitress.

"Good choice," Jeanne said. "In fact, I'll split mine with you. You can split yours with me when it comes." She put half on her bread plate and slid it over. He looked at her. The smile came back. He took her salad fork and dug in.

★★★

They talked while they ate, enjoying the food, the conversation becoming more familiar as he explained his disappearance. He said he had managed to stagger in the wind and rain to the Rover, and once inside used the GPS unit to learn with great surprise that he was on Hilton Head Island. He said that while sitting there, he tried to think what he was doing on the Island, and with whom, but drew a blank.

He remembered his home address, however, and after checking his license to make sure the address matched, entered it into the GPS unit. With the unit providing directions, he began his journey home. And after naps at rest stops and a night in a motel, he arrived the next day. He laughed after he told her the relief he felt when he pushed the garage-door button on the dashboard and the door opened. He laughed louder after he said a key on the key ring opened a door into the house.

Well that certainly explains what happened," she said, nodding slowly. "Why … how … what … Back then, I went a little crazy trying to make sense of it all."

"Glad I could be of service, ma'am," he offered, making an

opening hands gesture. "And now that I've satisfied your curiosity, could you satisfy mine? Tell me about the three days before I left."

With minimum detail, she explained quickly how they had met on the beach, her invitation to dinner, that one thing had led to another in the midst of the looming hurricane, and that he had spent three days in her condo after learning the hotel was closing.

"My turn," she said before he could ask for specifics. "Tell me why, after three months, you came back down here?"

"My doctor recommended it. I knew from a credit card bill that I stayed at this hotel during my lost week. He said that coming back here might help me. Particularly if I could find someone down here who knew me and could share what they knew. He said that memories that surfaced as a result might help my brain repair itself."

He told her that when he returned to work he found that occasional short-term memory failures occurred. Also that planning and organizing were more difficult than before. And that when problems happened, he had trouble controlling his emotions. He said the anger that occurred didn't last, but the depression that followed did. He added that all of that ruled out any kind of relationship with a woman.

"Things have improved though ... somewhat," he added. "The headaches are mostly gone. Never have a seizure. Still having problems sleeping, though. Small noises wake me and I can't get back to sleep."

"Are you taking anything?"

"My doctor doesn't recommend sleeping pills. Prefers small doses of anti-depressant medication. Half hour before bed."

"What kind of doctor was that ... a neuro something?"

"Neuropsychologist. Has advanced training in how brain injuries affect behavior. What tests are needed. What treatment strategy is preferred ..."

Jeanne nodded understandingly, then, lips pursed, stared absently out at the beach for a long moment and remembered the three days and how much she had liked this man. And by nature a giving person, there seemed only one road to take. "Well, if sharing what I remember about our time together will help, I'm game."

His dish arrived. They finished it, ordered and ate desert. Afterward, they agreed to meet at noon the next day, and said goodnight.

★★★

They met in the hotel lobby. After brief hellos she led him out to the beach to the spot where they had first met and then along the beach on the same path as before. He listened as she steered the conversation to what she remembered of their discussion that first day.

"Anything come to mind?" she asked at the end of the path. "Any memories?"

He shook his head slowly, concentrating, trying, but not remembering.

She took his hands, held them, looked up in his eyes. "This is where I invited you to dinner … at my condo." She repeated the invitation. "And it's for real this time, too."

He felt warmth from her hands and kindness from her eyes flow up into his brain, generating mental activity. The activity, in turn, forming new synapses, connecting nerve cells the head injury had disconnected. He closed his eyes, stood motionless, and concentrated. She did not interrupt.

Half a minute passed, then abruptly, "I remember something," he said. His eyes opened and he looked at her.

"Oh boy," she said, looking back at him.

"Excitement," he told her. "I remember standing here and feeling excited. No words, just the sensation."

She nodded. "It's a start. More will come."

"Lunch?"

"Love to."

His eyes narrowed. He looked away for a moment and then back. "You like pizza don't you?"

"I do," she answered. "Was that a memory or a guess?"

He shook his head slowly. "I don't know. It just popped out. Without thinking."

"I'm putting it in the memory column. That's two and we're just getting going."

"I like the optimism and ... you too."

The pizza in the hotel restaurant was delicious but evoked no new memories. Afterward, she invited him for dinner at her condo. She gave him the address, and he entered it in his phone. They parted in the hotel lobby after a quick hug and her promise of new memories. "A lot of them ..."

★★★

Jeanne's condo bell rang at six o'clock. She opened the door and saw Paul. He held out a dozen roses. "On the way over here I had this thought that you love roses," he said. "Third in the column? ... I hope?"

"Third it is," she said, taking the flowers. "I do love them, and just like now, you brought me some when you came by that first evening."

He followed her into the kitchen. She found a vase and put the flowers in it. "I cooked a steak just like this that first night," she said, pointing to a boneless strip steak, cut in half, sitting on paper towels on the counter. "Two pounds."

"I think I remember the taste of that steak," he said, staring at it. "Maybe number four?"

"Let's find out." She used tongs to place both pieces in a smoking hot cast-iron skillet on her stove. "You do the honors," she added, handing him the tongs. "Flip them every thirty seconds ... just like you did that first night. Add salt and pepper after every other flip."

She took a bowl of mashed potatoes and one of green beans warming in the oven and brought them into the dining room. Then she took dishes and silverware from a hutch and set the table. When she went back to the kitchen, the steaks had contracted in size and the crust had turned dark brown.

"Almost done," she said. "I'll take it from here. You pour the wine. Cabernet in the fridge. Napa Valley."

A couple minutes later they were seated at the table with the food served and the wine poured. Paul, who had said little since mentioning he remembered the taste of that first-night steak, stared at his plate. Then Jeanne watched him take his knife and fork, and with deliberation, cut a thin slice off the steak and eat it.

He smiled at her. "Exactly as I remembered," he said, savoring the flavor. "Definitely one for the column." She returned the smile.

They ate in silence, enjoying the food, the steak in particular. To break the ice she asked what he had done that afternoon.

"Used my laptop to answer about 50 emails," he said, adding, "Work-related. Nothing personal."

She knew what he was saying but asked anyway. "Nothing to any ... significant other ..."

"Like I said before, the craziness rules out any kind of relationship. I've tried, but just when things start moving forward, I'll do something weird that ruins it."

After the dinner and wine Jeanne noticed Paul lose the thread of their conversation. He knew it also, said he felt a headache coming on and should go back to the hotel. She countered, offered her guest room. He accepted, helped her with the dishes, said he was tired and went into the guest room.

She shook her head as the door closed behind him. *Not how we spent our first night together.*

★★★

Jeanne heard the guest room shower running around ten o'clock the next morning. A few minutes later Paul came into the kitchen.

"How do you feel?" she asked.

"Well rested," he replied, then looked at his watch. "Which makes sense since I slept about twelve hours."

"I'm glad. Need you wide awake to add to that column."

"Ah yes, the memory column. Left it at four if I remember right."

"We'll start working on it as soon as you've eaten some breakfast," she said. "Pancakes or eggs? I have both ready."

"I'm sorry. Don't you have to go to work?"

Her look of surprise turned to concern. "It's Saturday …"

He looked again at his watch then nodded slowly. "So it is. Subtract one from the column."

It wasn't easy, but as they repeated the activities of that earlier visit as best as she could remember them, the column rose in number far more than it dropped. So much so that Sunday evening he convinced her to take a few days off so they could finish and do it all over again. Which they did, and this time … all the activities. And at the end of the second round, he swore to her that his mind and memory had returned to normal.

And years later they would look back on this time as the wildly imperfect beginning of what would become their perfect lifetime romance.

Rachelle Jeffery

The Burden

John MacIlroy

It was just where he had left it, the small town of his childhood.

He hadn't been back in years, and likely wouldn't have gone except for Hurricane Matthew, a most unwanted visitor to his cottage along a tidal marsh in Bluffton. An early October nightmare, it rudely bounced along the southeastern coast, a drunken sailor of a storm that slapped almost headlong into the home he and his wife had shared since moving to the Lowcountry a decade earlier. Together, they had come to love the quiet rhythm of the marsh, until a blood clot took her away ten months earlier. The clot had been lurking deep and silently within her, as deadly as those tics in the gentle breezes off the coast of Africa that roll west, and can turn ugly.

★ ★ ★

The storm, sometime after midnight, felled the two live oaks that had stood guard by the cottage for almost a century. Their branches had draped gracefully over much of the house, wisps of Spanish moss just kissing the green tin roof. His wife often said the canopy made her feel safe, that it reminded her of the *church and steeple* her young interlocked fingers had formed when she was hunkered down in her family's storm shelter, dark clouds on her native Kansas horizon, her family in prayer. His hands had clutched only a cell phone and flashlight when the trees smashed through the back porch.

He had been a fool to ride it out.

At the peak of the storm, sometime around three-thirty in the morning, the French doors—the old kind that opened inward—blew. The rain drilled almost horizontally into the living room for hours. It spared only a few of the marital treasures his wife had so carefully arranged in the white bookcases which lined the wall—their son's Southern Miss college mug, their daughter's wedding picture, and a smoky orange juggling pin they bought at a flea-market early in their marriage, a treasure with its a curious faded sticker reading *"Birkenbach Sporting Goods, 'It Pays to Play,' Columbus, Ohio."*

★ ★ ★

He left his cottage a week later, one of the lucky ones to find a contractor who could begin repairs right away. The death of his wife, and now the storm, had set him adrift, an old man waiting for his compass to settle down, unsure of how to fill the next weeks. He thought of driving south, a daughter in Sarasota and a son in Tampa.

But the weather was still fine up north, and he headed instead to the small town of his youth, a village really along the forgotten west branch of the Raritan River in northern New Jersey.

★ ★ ★

Pulling off Route 22, just beyond Vaux Hall, he saw it, the Rock which loomed over the northern edge of town, and even larger in local lore. Rising some five-hundred feet, almost vertically, its sheer face the scar tissue left behind from some early trap-rock quarry operation, the Rock was nestled between the first and second ridges of the Watchung Mountains. But the boyhood magic of the place was an open-sided building, maybe the size of a two-car garage, set atop the Rock in a small clearing. Built of chestnut at the turn of the last century as a picnic shelter, the Lookout was a rustic local treasure. It offered sweeping views of his town to the south, as well as the tracks of the old Lackawanna curving west toward Summit and east toward the hint of the New York skyline, at least on a clear day.

And it was just scary enough to stir the imagination of every kid in town.

A wobbly chain-link fence wandered tentatively along the ledge of the cliff, a yard or so from the Lookout. Mothers for generations had warned their kids not to press the fence, just as generations of kids had dared and doubled-dared each other to do exactly that. Everyone simply figured the local Thursday-only paper, the *News-Item*, would someday scream the headline: *"IDIOT BOYS FOUND SMASHED AT BOTTOM OF THE ROCK, DIDN'T LISTEN TO THEIR MOTHERS."*

But something was wrong.

He squinted to see the Lookout. He knew exactly where to look, at the eastern corner of the sheer face.

It wasn't there.

★ ★ ★

He took his first trip to the Rock when he was five, piling into the family second-hand, four-door Packard, an awful teal green which looked worse *after* it was waxed, awful colors the sad burden of buying from the available inventory off the used car lot in Union.

The Packard had joined his family in the declining years of its design, all rounded and soft and puffy and crowned with a hood emblem that looked like the chrome handle off some new GE appliance. The car rolled around on oversized, even bulbous, white-wall tires. The whole thing shouting *clown car*. His family, not the stuff of contrarians, willingly bought into the suburban program pretty much as presented by others in charge, silly cars of the left-over sort leading the way.

In the back of the car a picnic basket served as the DMZ between brother and sister, keeping a shaky peace. Both were world-class fidgets, quick to squirm and roam the tan-grey back seat, which smelled like a damp rug in a cigarette factory. The back seat also sported a delightful chorus of intriguing stains, shouting years of untethered kids. The most recent was a real beauty, a small handprint spilling over the edge of the seat, driver's side, in a fading peanut-butter-and-grape-jelly purple, likely Welch's.

The drive to the top of the Rock took less than half an hour, or two parental cigarettes—each—in Kent time. The picnic lunch was made from scratch: fried chicken, macaroni, potato salads, carrot sticks, and chocolate cookies. And always the deviled eggs. Everything packed neatly in a sturdy dirty-blond wicker basket along with cloth napkins, a checkered red-and-white tablecloth, real silverware, and a couple of thermos bottles of lemonade with maroon-red twist off caps.

On that first trip to the top of the Rock, his dad also took a crack at the history of the place. During the Revolution, it was one of some twenty signal stations built by Washington to observe the movement of British troops quartered on Manhattan, and his dad spun a gripping tale of the British push westward, in June of 1780, toward Washington's troops hunkered down in Morristown.

In short, the place was the real deal, as was much of the promise of the American Dream back then, in small towns like his across the land.

★ ★ ★

After the "Family Picnic Era," which lasted for five or six years, most of his trips to the Lookout were on foot. But the real fun started when he got his license and could drive up there, park off Crest Drive, and walk a gentle path down to the Lookout. It was a surprisingly romantic place for a young man with a Jersey driver's license, particularly if he had the gift of historical insight and imagination and could spin to a young lady a riveting tale of some scared and tired young soldier in Washington's army firing off the signal to save the day in 1780.

He, however, did not have that gift.

What he did have was a third-hand 1957 Chevy. It had become the second family car sometime late in his seventeenth year, a slightly punch-drunk, milk-white four door mess of a car. It was as heavy as a tank, with patched red seats, runaway chrome bumper blight, a front floorboard rusted to a wafer-thin *idea* of a floorboard on the passenger side, and a steering wheel as large as the rims on his first bicycle. After he left for college, some guy who had taken the bus over from Newark bought the car, twenty bucks exchanged in the driveway, the guy so happy with his first car that he said he was going to fix it up and keep it forever.

A 1957 Chevy! Twenty bucks! Sure hope he did, those fixed-up '57

Chevys at last year's Concours on Hilton Head worth thousands, and who knows how much when forever arrives.

* * *

Late in the fall of their senior year, he drove to the top of the Rock with his girlfriend, a preppy day-student at the tony Kent School in the town next door. He remembered a bright, crisp day as they walked hand-in-hand down the short path to the Lookout, the pleasing crunch of the leaves under their feet even if the colors were well-beyond their earlier golden prime. It had become their special place, talk up there unhurried and often deep, and they were ready to leave their mark, initials inside a heart, carved into the seasoned chestnut wood of the old structure. This ritual had been going on for generations, the whole place looking like those ancient heavy wooden tables in most college-town bars, carved to near collapse with other testaments to young love.

Another couple was up there too, which added a nice touch. He found a spot on a post along the east-facing side, shoulder level, his old Boy Scout knife soon hard at work. It took a while, but his effort was rewarded with a gentle kiss and an unspoken understanding that *nothing could be more forever than . . . well, the two of them.* They thought their carving as sacred as those paintings found along the walls of those deep caves in France, around Dordogne. It was a sweet moment, even by his fumbling standards, marvelously in tune with the tides of young love, at once mysterious and innocent and forgiving.

But mostly trusting in the magic of *forever.*

* * *

It's just that forever is the stuff of dreams, and seventeen-year-olds.

His girl dumped him for a Phi Gam from a small school in New Hampshire soon after they both left for college, a little less than a year later. When he came home for Thanksgiving he slipped up to the Lookout, once again with his old Boy Scout knife, a habit he had yet to break. It was quiet up there, and lonely. A cold, late afternoon mist swirled around him, and even he got some of those historical willies. He stared at the post he still thought of as *theirs*, surprised that someone had already nibbled at the edge of their initials, the heart now looking more like a liver, his initials trespassed by the carving of some other young lover. Taking the knife from his pocket, he quickly chipped away at what was left of his initials. Then, painfully remembering just how precisely her *Dear John* letter had written her new boyfriend's fraternity letters, he carved those Greek letters in their place. It was truly pointless, maybe even a sacrilege to the Greek Sacred Order. But at that moment, high above the childhood town he had already begun to leave, he thought it an act of exquisite balance and romantic legend, like cutting off an ear, but not so disfiguring.

He tossed the old knife off the cliff, into the cold mist.

And then he wept.

★　★　★

He had always thought he would return to the Lookout, taking his wife along. It would have been the kind of journey we sometimes take to find—clues of who we were, once, and maybe even why. But sometime in the 1980s the Lookout was torn down, replaced, as he learned in town later that day, by a cold concrete platform. Rumor has it that the old chestnut posts and beams had gotten weak, the whole thing shaky and perching too close to the cliff face, which was eroding away too.

No, he whispered to himself, that's not what happened at all. The old structure just couldn't bear the sweetly sad weight of all those lost forevers and broken hearts, and collapsed of its own sad burden.

The Funny Side

Donna Varner

Sansing McPherson

Strawberry Moon

Sansing McPherson

The Summer Solstice—the longest day, the highest arc, the richest sunshine—wedded with the full moon in June 2016. This full moon had an exquisite name—the Strawberry Moon, so called by the Algonquin tribe for the time to harvest strawberries. Lois was not about to miss it. Summer Solstice always struck an enchanted chord for her of pagan rituals, bonfires, and Thomas Hardy heaths. It also begins the shortening of days, which made her strangely glad and sad together, as if she were about to lose something held dear.

Her husband, Ed, had been in a deep funk lately, and, hoping it would cheer him up, she persuaded him to make the short walk to see the moon rising over Port Royal Sound. Behind them the trees at Dolphin Head point hid the sunset, but the eastern sky was an evening-soft pink and blue. At the mouth of the sound by the Atlantic they spied diamond-bright lights on dredging boats that anchored there at night after renourishing Hilton Head Island's beaches all day.

As Ed grumbled and swatted no-see-ums—devilish little Lowcountry bloodsuckers—a gleaming edge peeked over the ocean horizon. The moon ascended steadily into a rosy orb directly over the boats.

"I've never seen a grander, more brilliant moon," Lois cried. "It really is strawberry red!" She held her breath, and when she began to breathe again, she felt an endorphin rush.

She glanced at Ed. His normally dour mouth had managed two up-turned corners. "Nice," he said.

She snapped a dozen photos that, when uploaded, gave her two she could be proud of. She deleted the rest—fuzzy red-orange basketballs above a blurry ocean. For days afterward people posted their own gorgeous photos of the strawberry moon on Facebook.

The photos sank down to the depths of her Facebook timeline, and endorphins drained as Ed began to feel worse. His doctor ordered lab work.

Lois had forgotten her cell phone when she went shopping the day the lab results came back. She returned home in the early afternoon to find a hand-written scrawl.

"Joe drove me to ER. Come ASAP."

Her husband of forty-five years was near kidney failure.

Ominous thoughts loomed like the leafy oaks and Spanish moss that hovered above the road as she rushed to Hilton Head Regional Hospital. Would she and Ed ever walk to the sound path together and watch a full moon rise again? They had just celebrated their forty-fifth anniversary. She had hoped for at least fifty.

They spent ten uncertain hours in an ER ward, Ed on a lumpy gurney, and Lois on a wooden straight-back chair. It was midnight before he got a room. That this was not in ICU was a plus, but they still had not seen a doctor beyond the emergency room staff. Could they view that as a not-a-crisis sign?

At 12:45 a.m., yawning, bleary-eyed, and trying to get to sleep in more comfortable furnishings—Ed in a hospital bed with crisp white sheets and Lois in a brown vinyl recliner—a wild-haired, little old man wearing a fishing vest shuffled into Ed's room. He had either come straight from the streets, a frog-gigging pond, or Middle Earth.

This, it turned out, was the nephrologist, the brilliant Yoda who explained, smiled, reassured, and crunched blood chemistry numbers constantly to adjust Ed's IV meds. The next morning they met the charming young urologist, who lost all charm when he ordered a catheter.

As best Lois could tell, the closest thing to labor that a man can endure is having a catheter inserted. Her dear one wore that device for ten days before his kidneys were pronounced well. They became statistical geeks about creatinine levels and urine output, sharing the numbers with friends who had only called to wish Ed well.

Given that it was ninety-five degrees outside, the hospital air conditioning was really cranked, and Ed was constantly cold. His room was on the north side of the building, and the sun never shone directly in. The wonderful nursing staff brought him warm cotton blankets, each barely one millimeter thick. That's why they had to bring three at a time.

When he started to emerge from misery and the kidneys were definitely on the mend, Lois and Ed began to walk the halls together, increasing the distance each day. He pushed his pet giraffe, the IV pole, while she made sure a blanket stayed around his shoulders and the one-size-fits-all hospital gown didn't gape in the back.

"Isn't there anywhere I can get warm?" he asked one day, pale, pitiful, and shivering.

Lois knew a place. For over a week she'd roamed every hall, memorized every floor tile, admired every piece of student art as she walked while he napped. The hallway to the emergency room wing had large east-facing, full-length windows that overlooked the leafy Memory Garden, beautiful to behold from the second story.

As they turned down the hallway, they felt the air warming. The large sunny windows in the distance drew them like moths to a porch light. He pushed his giraffe faster. She followed in a stoop, trying to keep his gown closed in the back, noting that his poor keister was rosy red from so much time in bed.

At last they were there.

"Aah," he said and flattened the entire front side of his body against the warm window glass. He stood there, eyes closed, smiling blissfully for nearly five minutes before he turned and pressed the other side against the glass.

While he toasted in the sun, she admired the garden below and noticed a family approaching from a distance to visit the tranquil place.

They drew closer.

She looked at Ed, obliviously warm and happy.

She looked at his gown. It gaped. Against the glass window.

Strawberry moon.

Fashion News – Real Headlines – Well-Versed

Norm Levy

AT 57, BARBIE GETS A NEW BODY.
COMES IN TALL, CURVY AND PETITE

Associated Press

Barbie, the iconic plastic doll, whose small waist and long legs have been criticized for creating unrealistic expectations for girls, will soon be sold with three new bodies – curvy, tall and petite.

In the REAL world, one can only gripe,
That they CAN'T change their body type.

REVENGE OF THE ANTI-HANDBAG
(BIG LOGOS ARE OUT)

The Wall Street Journal

They're not flashy or hyped. No one is begging celebrities to lug them about. But these discreetly chic carry-alls—from Mansur Gavriel, the Row, A.P.C. and more—are quietly wooing women in the know.

If it flaunts a huge logo, don't flag it.
If it hypes a designer, just BAG IT.

FASHION PRISM BREAK –
RETRO LOOK OF RAINBOW STRIPES

The Wall Street Journal

Many designers are opting for variegated stripes on everything from knits to stiletto pumps. The trend must be exquisitely executed to override the Kitsch factor.

Where will the fashion urbane go?
"Somewhere over the rainbow."

BLUE JEANS LOSING THEIR GRIP ON AMERICAN HIPS

NPR

Seems the nation is leisurizing its pants, bypassing the dungarees and choosing elastic waistbands and sweats instead. Sales of yoga pants and other active wear climbed.

Elastic waistbands and baggy sweats,
Are now the "fitting" silhouettes.

HIGH FASHION CLOUT- SANDALS SO UGLY, THEY'RE CHIC

The Wall Street Journal

What's chic, and has all the chic of an orthopedic shoe? A host of new designer sandals for summer and fall. It may be one of the stranger high-fashion trends in recent memory: the flat, broad sandal, so clumsy that it's downright "fugly," to use the term that fashion bloggers have adopted.

Wisdom of the footwear boutique;
If it's ugly, "turn the other chic!"

Gretchen Nickel

Prescription

Barry Dickson

Feeling a pain deep inside,
or occasional emptiness?
Consider taking poetry.

(Those who are pregnant or could become pregnant
should read poetry with caution. Poetry can cause
you to do things that might make you pregnant.
Poetry can alter the shape of your heart.
In some cases, successfully publishing poetry has caused swelling of the head.
Poetry makes people see things that aren't really there.
It can cause drowsiness, and reactions to certain poetry
have been misdiagnosed as narcolepsy.
Poetry has been linked to mood swings—weeping to fits of laughter.
Do not mix poetry with alcohol, the poet has taken care of that.
Certain people have severe reactions to poetry. In critics, for example,
it can provoke nastiness and impaired judgment.
Cases of Tourette's have been reported, readers blurting out "Huh?"
or "What the hell does that mean?"
If poetry results in an erection lasting more than four hours,
consult a hot English teacher.)

Ask your doctor if poetry is right for you!

Duncan McPherson

Tie Food

Gene Youtz

I opened the box shelved in the guest room closet and lo and behold I had saved my favorites—fourteen in all, not including the one that lights up when you squeeze it in the vital spot. I know that during my working lifetime I had accumulated close to a couple of hundred of these draperied adornments. Now, after having given away at least seventy-five to my friend Berdie for her children to do with what they may at daycare, and another equal amount to Goodwill, plus some that got left or lost, I was reduced to a fortnight's worth—the cream of the crop you might say.

Push had come to shove, and I would have to choose just the right one for our upcoming mini reunion with friends we hadn't seen since college, more than fifty years ago.

It was all Thack's idea that I was in this hang-up. I had told him that I don't wear neckties anymore because I don't have to. He said that he rather enjoyed getting dressed for dinner. I had no more suits either, I explained, just a few leftover sport coats that didn't get tossed in the great leap to South Carolina. He said he thought that ought to be fine—it was easy to see why Thack had worked in public relations all those years. The plan was to gather in Charleston for the weekend—Thack, our wives, both of whom are named Barbara, and me. Both couples would have a two-and-a-half-hour drive coming from opposite directions—they from barely into coastal North Carolina, and we from the Lowlands, just a few miles north of the Georgia border.

We would be dining at Peninsula Grill, one of Charles Towne's best. It was recommended by Thack's friend and neighbor Max, who indicated that the restaurant most likely required coat and tie. Not wanting to be a party poop and thankful to Max for recommending the eatery, not to mention having gotten us incredible off-season hotel rates, I acquiesced and began looking for just the right neckwear.

As I sorted through my collection, I was reminded of Luigi's Trattoria—a wonderful Washington D.C. pizza parlor (which is still there) where, in the late 50s, we students would gather after a week of classes at American University. There, in the back dining room, was a collection of ties attached to the wall, mostly going back to the 40s. The original Mr. Luigi apparently delighted in sneaking up on an unsuspecting customer with a pair of large scissors, whereupon he would lop off the guy's tie just below the knot. Of course, the ties looked pretty awful, having hung there collecting grease and dust over the years. I cogitated a similar arrangement for my collection, but quickly thought better of it.

One of my favorite ties was gone however. I can't even describe it other than it was posh and I wore it on a sales call to see Milt who headed up a national educational association. He took one look at the tie and told me how sharp it was. I thanked him and continued talking, whereupon he said again that he really liked my tie. So I said, "Do you want it?" He said that he did, and so I took it off and gave it to him. He kept it for a year and then one day gave it back with a card of thanks. It made me wonder if I might be able to start a tie lending mart.

My remaining crop of ties are works of art—literally. Not only that, but like the one I gave to Milt, we have history together. My favorite, and the one that always got raves, is a color-exploded abstract that I bought on K Street from a sidewalk vendor for two dollars. There are none with stripes, but I have ties with parrots, the Flintstones, multiple chefs, and bicycles (from Amsterdam). Then there are the obligatory repetitive diagonal patterns of Maine whales and Maryland crabs—scenes from the Carnival of Venice and grape picking time in Napa Valley. And there are those by famous artists such as Tiffany, Seurat, and Klee.

But the one that caught my attention which I ultimately chose to travel to Charleston with, is a combination of the above features—small classic repetitive diagonal pattern—famous artist—

bought at a major European art museum. It was early afternoon December 31, 1997, in Madrid, and we had just landed and gone to our hotel with friends Carolyn and Phil. We checked into our rooms, and then at about 3:30 p.m. we re-gathered in the lobby, deciding to walk down the street to the Museo del Prado. By the time we arrived, we would have just about an hour to rush through this expansive museum. We made a cursory tour seeing a myriad of old masters, including the Spaniards, Velazquez, El Greco, and of course Francisco Goya, whose *La Maja Desnuda* is one of the most renowned paintings in the world—for obvious reasons. We topped off the visit with a stop, just before 5:00 p.m., in the gift shop. As I strolled around, with the intercom warning of a closing in five minutes, I felt a tug on my sleeve to find Barbara pointing to a particular neck tie. Why, of course it was *The Naked Maja*—or rather an orderly cluster of aslant tiny couched pink naked ladies peppered in perfect precision on a field of blue. I bought it. And now twelve years later here I was preparing to take her away with me to Charleston. But how come I chose this tie, I pondered? There must be a connection with our visit.

It occurred to me that I might find some answers from the Internet, and so I thought, "I'll just Google her." I did so and discovered that this lady's identity was a mystery. Depending upon who you believe, she was either the 13th Duchess of Alba, or perhaps Pepito de Tudo, an artist's model. Others speculate that she is actually a composite of a number of models. I prefer to believe that she is the Duchess—rumored to have been Goya's paramour—whose given name is Maria, which in some languages is Maya. Whoever she was, her likeness certainly created a scandal in Madrid at the end of the 18th century—to the point that a few years later Goya painted the same figure with clothes on. But this didn't seem to satisfy The Spanish Inquisition, which in 1815 demanded to know who commissioned him to paint such an obscenity. He refused to say and was removed from his position in the Spanish Court. That wasn't the end of it, for in 1930 a pair of privately produced stamps of *The Maya* were accepted by Spain's

Postal System; however, the U.S. didn't approve and barred all mail with these stamps from entering our country.

But this still didn't speak to the lady's connection with Charleston. I searched again and this time hit pay dirt (so to speak). Seems as though it had to do with Spoleto—a small town in Italy, but also a music festival begun in 1977 in Charleston at the behest of Gian Carlo Menotti, who sought an American connection to emulate his venue in Italy. It was an instant success and remains so until this day, running for two and half weeks from late May through mid-June. By the time the festival began Menotti had long since established himself in the world of opera, and in 1986 he was honored to have his new opera, *Goya*, commissioned by Madrid-born Placido Domingo in the title role, premiere at the Kennedy Center in Washington D.C. It bombed.

But luckily for him, Menotti revised the score and in 1991 it was performed at Spoleto in Charleston. That version has been recorded and is available today. So, there was the connection— the story of Goya's life, featuring the Duchess of Alba. The only thing I don't know is whether either version included a naked lady—I'm told no, but without a libretto to follow I have no way of knowing. If *Goya* ever returns to Spoleto, I shall be at the ready with my *La Maja Desnuda*.

We had arrived in the city shortly before noon and caught up with Thack and Barbara soon after. We spent the afternoon variously lunching, walking, window shopping, and reminiscing. By the end of the day we returned to our hotel to prepare for an 8:00 p.m. dinner.

As I dressed for the evening, I pondered whether I would be able to tie up my *Naked Maja* into a proper double Windsor knot. Surprisingly (like riding a bike I suppose) I finished her off on the first try; proper length and all, with the small end shorter than the wide end. The only thing missing was a tie protector such as the one given me by Lynn, a client and friend with whom I had lunched often during my sales tenure and who was aware of my propensity for littering my ties with food. The device consisted of an appropriate sized clear plastic sheet (with tiny yellow dots) which rolled up into a metal tube with a clip, made to be whipped out and attached to one's tie just below the knot and then pulled down like a window blind. Then, after the meal, it could be wiped off and rolled back up for future use. Barbara had suggested that I take it, but alas it had gotten lost somewhere along the line, and now I would be reduced to using *Maya* as a food protector for my shirt.

When we got to the restaurant I immediately began looking to see if any of the gentlemen were sans tie. Well, there was every form of dress code represented from open-necked sport shirt to turtle neck under a coat (this guy reminded me of my similar attempt in the 60s to buck the tie code). There were sport coats with no ties and sport coats with ties, and some few with suit and tie. So, there it was—the new America—true democracy. No more uniforms, not even in this once-fortress city that harkens back to the bona fide ante-bellum South.

We were seated, and finally I was able to display my neck-wear. I sat up straight, chest out, to show off the tie to Thack and Barbara. They smiled politely and then I realized that from their vantage point the images were too small to be seen. Subtlety had trumped sex, so I held the tie out for them to more easily see it's true nature whereupon they chuckled and I was then able to segue into the history of the painting as well as the connection to Charleston.

When we got home on Sunday, I unpacked her highness, and sure enough I had managed to dribble food on her. I carefully wiped the orts off of her ladyship's multiplicity to make her clean again and ready for her next adventure. Almost as an afterthought, I checked Wikipeda to see if they had anything further to add to my newfound Goya knowledge. In the very first paragraph they say that *The Naked Maya* "... is sometimes said to be the first clear depiction of female pubic hair in a large Western painting." Well fancy that—here I had assumed that all of those female nude statues and paintings, done throughout the Renaissance, of various lady's glabrous loins, were the result of prudish artists or vitamin deficiency or perhaps even Papal Decree. Now, thanks to Francisco, I know the difference between nude and naked—in English anyway.

Independence Days

~

Tom Crawford

In 2012, Jan Maganini, activities director of The Seabrook, the first Continuing Care Retirement Community on Hilton Head Island, took a census to find out how many residents of the community, tucked next to the Sea Pines resort on the southern tip of the island, were ninety-five and older. A few residents conducted a poll at their table at dinner. Guesses ranged from six to ten of the total residence population of approximately 250.

They, and Jan herself, were astounded at the survey results. There were twenty-eight names on the list. And not all of them were pleased when Jan announced a party to recognize longevity.

Most of them were more proud of their vitality than their longevity.

Few of their number were residents of the Fraser Health Center, the Seabrook's adjacent nursing facility. Most still lived independently.

Barbara O'Connor, a resident member of the Seabrook Board of Directors, provided three prescriptions for healthy senior living at an apartment cocktail party to welcome new arrivals. They were good nutrition, lack of stress and wholesome activities.

Most of the stress was outside the gates of The Seabrook after the recession beginning in 2008. There was the plunging stock market, falling interest rates, and lower commercial and residential property prices. The Seabrook responded by turning no longer desired artist studios into one-bedroom apartments, and by leasing apartments donated by long-term residents who had died, moved out or transferred into the nursing home.

The first census revealed that where there had been one centenarian at the Seabrook in 2012, by August 2016 there were eight. Three died during the next few months, but two more were added, making a total of seven. Whereas there were twenty-eight residents ninety-five or older in 2012, the tally in 2017 was thirty-six. A separate tally of residents more than ninety years of age was ninety, with eighty-five living independently, and only five residents in the Fraser Health Center.

But the most stressful event of the period was Hurricane Matthew. How would the aging residents, now including centenarians, take that? Several accounts follow.

Helen Rankin is one hundred two at this writing and is still going strong. After a lengthy career as a registered nurse in Indiana, New York state, and Massachusetts, she moved into the Seabrook in 1994. She hardly retired. During the next two decades, she continued to share her nursing career experience as a volunteer at the Hilton Head Hospital. This iron lady had donated 20,000 hours of her time to this service.

It served well during hurricane Matthew. The Seabrook had to execute its evacuation plan on very short notice in October, 2016. Nevertheless, many things jelled during that exodus to Orangeburg for those who had placed their fortunes on The Seabrook. Helen Rankin, who is quite hard of hearing, found her new roommate for the next eight days also turned out to be a nurse, with sight problems.

Evie (Tommie) Ellis, one hundred two, was blind in one eye and had only ten percent vision in the other. But she also had a support from which only two of the centenarians at the Seabrook benefited. Her son, Charles Ellis, seventy-four, an orthodontist, had moved in to assist his aging mother.

During her career in nursing and as a stewardess with Atlantic Airlines, Tommie had lived in Mississippi, Tennessee, New York City, New Orleans and North Carolina, before moving to The Seabrook in September of 1998. Her son's move had enabled her to remain in her apartment for nearly two decades.

But hurricane Matthew and the evacuation brought a change

to Tommie's routine. There was significant mingling with both members of the Seabrook staff and residents during the evacuation period. And there was one physical development.

"My voice changed," Tommie acknowledged good naturedly, "yelling at Helen."

Margaret (Meg) Hayes, like Tommie, enjoys the support of a son, the youngest of her four children, which has enabled her to remain in her apartment at The Seabrook for twenty-one years. She has lived in New York, Pennsylvania, New Jersey, Florida, North Carolina and Massachusetts, and was certified to teach special education in four states. But she seemed to have the most sparkle in her eyes when she talked about young children in her special education classes in Boston. Now, going on one hundred two, she regrets being chair-bound. Yet when she met a neighbor shortly after this interview, she also mentioned that she didn't remember the interviewer's name. The interviewer assured the neighbor that he would return to Meg's with a gift, with his name on it.

Suzanne (Sudie) Plowden, in her one hundred and second year, already has overcome two of life's blows that put many down. Texas-born and New Orleans bred, she graduated from Tulane University with a Bachelor of Fine Arts degree and pursued a lifetime of artistry for more than a half century. However, on a visit to Costa Rica, she broke her arm, a tragedy for an artist. But she recovered, and after dabbling in computer painting, she picked up her brushes again and produced, in her nineties, wonderful portraits of her daughter-in-law and grandson.

In November 2009, the death of her husband Ted, a Procter & Gamble sales executive whose assignments took the couple to five continents, was more difficult to handle. She slipped into a period of isolated sadness for a time until family, friends and Seabrook neighbors assisted her out of it.

At this writing, her apartment remains an exhibit of artistic scenes of Mumbai, India, South Africa, Brazil and Australia, plus dozens of portraits. Older magazine readers can recall Sudie and her twin sister, Lucerne Robert, recently deceased in South Africa, in the "Which Twin Has the Toni" ads of a half century ago. Both beauties are preserved on Sudie's canvasses. And Sudie is a regular at the Stretch 'n' Strengthen classes each week.

As for surviving hurricane Matthew, she remarks, "The aides were awfully good."

Richard James, the first male centenarian at The Seabrook, is 103. Richard was a career Navy pilot who was based in England, Morocco, Japan and Iceland overseas, and New Jersey, Florida, California, Kansas and Texas at home. He moved into The Seabrook in 2011. Richard astounds his neighbors with his up-to-date knowledge of current events despite severe limits on his vision which he overcomes through the use of modern devices.

His daughter and son-in-law, residents of nearby Sea Pines, provided escape from Matthew to Ninety Six, an upstate South Carolina community.

Helen Meighen is a native of Western Pennsylvania who has lived at The Seabrook since 2004. She and Martha Baumberger (now deceased), a retired foreign service officer in the U.S. State Department and the third mayor of Hilton Head Island, were the hostesses at this author's first invitation to dine at The Seabrook. Someone must have done some research because Helen's daughter Nancy and son-in-law Jack Biel, had both attended the same college as this writer, Westminster in New Wilmington, Pennsylvania. Jack turned out to be a member of the Board of Trustees of The Seabrook, and as a fellow alumnus and a lawyer, became the first to be retained in the Lowcountry. Helen lived at Waynesburg, Pittsburgh and Monongahela, Pennsylvania, and worked in the advertising department of the former Bell Telephone Company, tinting photographs. In retirement, she displayed her piano playing skills throughout her residence at The Seabrook, for worship services, variety shows and at her 100th birthday party.

Sam Mulrain served thirty-one years in the U.S. Army, retiring as a lieutenant colonel, was a plant manager for American Can Company, and worked twenty-five years as a starter at the Robert Trent Jones Golf Course at Palmetto Dunes on Hilton Head. Past ninety five, Sam was still playing a round or two of golf along with his starter duties at Palmetto Dunes. After that, he concentrated on the majority of ladies at the happy hours and in the dining rooms until he was ninety-nine, when he transferred to the Fraser Health Center, where he was still a distinct minority male. His foreign military tours were to Venezuela and France, and New York City, Jersey City, New Jersey; Patchogue, New York; Islip, Long Island; Berkley Heights, New Jersey; El Paso, Texas; and Memphis, Tennessee, served as home bases.

★ ★ ★

The deaths of three Seabrook centenarians took place after Maganini's census between November 2016 and March 2017. They were Alma Orr Cordle, Margaret Townsend Reid Downward and Helene Saul Parry.

Alma Orr Cordle
(April 12, 1913 – February 24, 2017)

Alma Cordle , who died on February 24, 2017, was one of too few Southern Belles at the Seabrook. She was born in Charlotte, North Carolina, was married in Charlotte, bore and raised five children in the Queen City and allowed only one to stray out of state, to Indiana. The five children, fifteen grandchildren and twenty-one great grandchildren survive. Also surviving is her longtime chief care giver, Verna Lowe-Ellis, who with other aides enabled her to remain in her apartment for seventeen years. She and her husband, Lew, who died on March 25, 2003, proclaimed they were active Democrats, and perhaps the only ones in their precinct. Besides politics, she also played tennis at the Sea Pines Club until she was ninety-four.

Margaret (Peg) Townsend Reid Downward
(July 6, 1914 – March 22, 2017)

Peg Townsend grew up in Pennsylvania. However, at age fourteen, after her father's death, Peg attended a boarding school far afield in Massachusetts, the Dana Hall School at Wellesley. She graduated from Vassar College in 1936 and married John Reid, a junior partner in a Washington law firm in 1939. Three children survive. Several years after Reid's death in 1984, Peg was reintroduced on Hilton Head to Jim Downward, to whom she had been briefly engaged before her first marriage. Downward and Peg, both widowed, married in 1993 and enjoyed seven years of marriage before his death in 2000. Peg lived independently at her Seabrook apartment for more than a decade before her move to the Fraser Health Center in her late nineties. She died there on March 22 at 102.

Helene Saul Parry
(October 29, 1911 – November 28, 2016)

Helene Parry was the first Seabrook resident to become a centenarian. She told one of her neighbors about the move to the Fraser that she was sick and tired of making her own breakfast.

Helene, who grew up in Chicago, became an academic peripatetic, studying at Columbia in New York, the London School of Economics, and the Zimmers International School in Geneva, Switzerland, before returning to the United States. She completed her academic studies at West Virginia University in Morgantown and Case Western Reserve University in Cleveland.

After careers with the War Department as a safety and security engineer and superintendent of public works in Norton, Virginia, she married George Parry, who was with the U.S. Bureau of Mines in West Virginia. They moved to Sea Pines on Hilton Head in 1962. She once showed a visitor at Fraser her itineraries of trips all over the United States and Europe with her husband,

and later while widowed with a female friend. These trips later continued all over the Seabrook campus in her wheelchair with or without companions, and her supply of reading material. She could be found on the wood walk, in gazebos and beside lagoons. She treasured her independence and her freedom.

She also left a list of Helenisms by which to live. These are just a few:

I left my gumption at home.

Bingo? I did that when I was three. Can't handle that now.

Fraser is easy to cope with—it allows a lot of freedom.

Helene (to her Aide): Do you have any other patients like me?
Aide: I don't know anyone else 105, and you are amazing.
Helene: It doesn't seem that way from here.

Life goes on; I tried to stop it, but it wouldn't stop.

It is easy to go blank. I can add anything there I want.

I am willing to die but can't give up the soup.

When Helene Parry finally gave up the soup on November 28, 2016, seven other residents of the Seabrook already had joined her in reaching the century mark.

Epilogue

Hurricane Matthew proved to be a unifying factor for the Seabrook in October of 2016. Most of the residents who had signed up for the Seabrook evacuation plan were transported to Orangeburg. Despite a one-day power outage in the central South Carolina city, most of the evacuees, staff, residents and patients were transported to safety with little difficulty.

What had been anticipated as a possible natural disaster had been transformed into an exciting adventure. Matthew had created a bond between residents and staff.

Fran Baer

Waiting for Sleep

Bill Newby

The tree line through the living room windows
looks like a giant with a bushy beard and bristled eyebrows
lying on his back and waiting like me for sleep
to draw its numbing fingers across our eyes.

But the sky is celebrating its freshwater delivery
with a light show sparked by rubbing its swollen breasts
across the earth's hairy thighs, and its fireworks
are like strobe light bursts of white energy and awareness,

nano-second illuminations of the porch railing,
tree trunks and lawn. Reminders that all is well,
the dull roar of rain hasn't disturbed the world,
and my vigilance is no longer necessary.

Judy Law Barnes

In Her Own Sweet Time

Bev Moss Haedrich

"Mom, who plays with him when we're not home?"

I thought for a moment, and said, "Well, um, that's when he sleeps."

"You sleep with dad, and I sleep with Pookie, Teddy and Starlight. So, who does he sleep with?!"

Hmm, this is going to be a tough one. Rhett, our feisty Springer, could be more than a bit stubborn at times. At a year and a half, I could swear he was either going deaf or had very selective hearing as simple *quiet* commands—even after Puppy Training, then Agility Training—were ignored. Granted, he was very protective of all of us. At least he barked loudly when someone approached our car, or when one of us was on a leisurely stroll with him in tow. But really, two Springers? What if his *new pal* was as rambunctious as him? Maybe, just maybe, a *female* would be the answer. *Worth a try*, I thought.

Over the years we had a variety of pets, some invited, others not. Dogs, however, would occupy our family for the next several years, beginning with an ADHD cocker spaniel named Toby—a striking blonde cocker that never found any peace in repose. One summer a neighbor's aunt and uncle were visiting from the Carolina mountains and spotted Toby running around the yard. They must have recognized Toby's anxiety and took an interest in him. They lived on ten splendid acres, and near the end of their visit, they asked if they could adopt him. They thought the energetic cocker and their free-roaming horses could be a perfect match. Toby jumped into the back seat of their SUV without hesitation. We stood there waving like idiots, hoping to capture his attention or a whiff of departing gratitude. But nary a coiffed ear turned in our direction. He was gone.

Then one day in a small shopping village near Shem Creek in Mt. Pleasant, my heart fluttered. I gasped.

"Is that a spaniel?"

"She sure is," the guy answered. "This is Molly. She's an English Springer Spaniel."

"What a cutie! How old is she?"

"She just turned twelve weeks yesterday." He picked her up, holding her infant legs in his palms. Her topaz eyes squinted at the bright sun. "Wanna hold her?"

I should have hesitated. I didn't. There she was, loving on me like I had just given her a favorite treat. *See, see how adorable I am?* Molly seemed to whisper as she found the lobe of my ear. *I could be your best friend and companion forever! And I won't ever have accidents in the house. Promise!* At this age, they're a bit light on loyalty.

Molly's owner handed me a scrap of paper with the breeder's name and phone number scribbled in blue ink. They lived about fifty miles south of Charleston, near Edisto. I think I still have that ragged-edged note among Rhett's things.

A visit was planned to meet the last male in the litter. Since the outcome was uncertain, I went alone. It would be easier than listening to a crying child who couldn't understand *why* he wasn't coming home with us.

The woman met me at her front gate. There he was. She held a beautiful, dark liver and brilliant white English Springer Spaniel with a single freckle on the side of his nose. He stretched out to sniff at me, his legs dangling in mid-air. I took him gently from her arms. *Just as cute as his sister.*

"So, you met his sister, did you?"

"Oh, yes. Molly. She's a doll baby for sure!"

The grassless run he played in was dusty, with yesterday's rain puddled at one end. *He deserves better than this,* I thought, laying the groundwork for my on-the-spot decision.

"He's the last one of the litter, and more than ready to go as you can see," she said, closing the gate behind us. "You could take him today, if you like."

As he settled onto my lap, I carefully backed out of the long driveway between the vibrant pink azaleas and beneath moss-laden oaks. The setting reminded me of one of the South's finest novels, *Gone With The Wind*. Right then and there, it just rolled off my tongue.

"Your name is Gentleman Rhett," I announced. He looked up at me, cuddled deeper into my lap and sighed. It was true that our suburban spread was no plantation, but I knew Rhett would find a happy life at our little Tara.

Over the next months Rhett graciously lived up to his name. The obedience and agility training reinforced his Southern charm. In class he could stand his ground with a stoic doberman pinscher towering over him, but getting Rhett to run through the flimsy tunnel was impossible. He'd run up ramps, jump through hoops, and walk across a raised platform. But the tunnel wasn't happening. He ignored me when I'd squirm into the opposite end of the tunnel, coaxing him to come. He chose to sit instead.

It was around the time of Rhett's first birthday I heard the question that would resurface many times, "So, who *does* Rhett sleep with?"

"Good question," I said.

I knew where this was going. My head understood the challenges of housebreaking and training along with the double cost of food, vet bills, toys, collars and leads, yet my heart was leading me in the same direction as my son's.

"Maybe he *would* like to have a friend when we're away." So there it was. The decision was made.

"Yes! We're getting a new puppy!"

"We'll call her Scarlett."

Each weekend we scrutinized breeders of new litters over hundreds of miles from the edge of Lowcountry marshes to deep country backroads in search of just the right lady for our gentleman. She, along with her parents, had to be dark liver and bright white.

"I'm calling about the puppies," I'd begin. "We're looking for a female to go with our liver and white male. She must be dark, very dark liver and white. And few freckles, if any."

Time and again we were assured they had *the* one for us, only to be disappointed when a litter of light shades of brown and off-white blends would come tumbling out, bouncing off one another for our attention. This would be no easy feat.

Several months later a classified ad changed our lives. When I phoned, the owner told me not only about the litter's mother and father, but the grandparents, too. She began interviewing *me*. Questions about our family. Our lifestyle. Why did we want one of their precious females? And, finally, would you like to come and see them?

Early Saturday morning I packed a lunch of egg salad sandwiches, chips and a few pickles for our sixty mile drive north. We turned into their pencil straight driveway and parked alongside a thick row of wax myrtles. Their home was elevated high above the waterline of nearby marshes.

"Hi! I'll meet you around back," she said, pulling her blonde hair up into a thin ponytail. "They're all expecting you!"

We walked slowly around the side of the house anticipating a burst of energy, but there was none. We stood in a huddle, enjoying the expansive view of the tall willowy marsh grass. I cupped a photo of Rhett in my hand, hoping one of their females would be Scarlett for our dashing Rhett.

"Chloe, here girl," she called out. The lactating mother strolled toward us. Even in her difficult state she had the energy to ward off the little ones in tow. She sat at our feet. We knelt down to pet her. The most gentle eyes gazed back at us. Her coat was smooth, and her coloring was exactly what we had scoured the coastline for these past months.

"Good girl! Don't let her calmness fool you. She comes from a long line of high jumpers."

"High jumpers?"

"Oh, yes. See the marks on the bark of that tree? That's where they play and get their exercise."

"You mean they jump that high!"

"Not only jump, they practically run up the tree to get their toy," her husband giggled as Chloe's ears perked up at the word *toy*. "No, not now, girl. And they're very competitive, too!"

"Come on, let's go over here and give her a break from her puppies," she said, picking up two of the fluffy balls of fur. The other four scrambled to keep up.

"They are so sweet!" we squealed. "Which ones are the females?"

"This is a female, and that one over there."

There she sat, tummy full of contentment, one paw under her small chest. She had no freckles! Her markings, excluding a fine white curved line on her right hip, were nearly identical to Rhett's. Her demeanor was calm and quiet.

"Hey there, little one," I cooed, carefully holding her up in the air for a better look. "How would you like to be named Scarlett?"

"Mom, she's the one! Look at her! She looks like Rhett! Let's take her home! Please!"

"Oh, she still has to stay with her mom awhile," I said, turning to the owner and handing her Rhett's picture. "What do you think? Can she be his Scarlett?"

She looked at her husband and they nodded in agreement. "She'll be perfect for Rhett."

The trip home went by fast as we talked about where she was going to sleep and what she could and could not eat. And, of course, how sweet and soft she was. But, most importantly, what would Rhett think of his new companion?

"She's so small! I know he'll be careful with her!"

"Oh, I'm sure he will. Scarlett is just five *weeks* old." Her name seemed a bit ill fitting for her now, but we knew she'd grow into it.

When we reached home, Rhett sniffed our shoes and began licking our fingers and hands.

"Look, Dad, he knows we've been playing with Scarlett!"

"He sure seems to, son."

"He does! Come on, Rhett, let's go outside," he said, opening the door to the backyard. "I'll tell you all about Scarlett! You're going to love her!"

A few weeks later when she and her siblings were weaned, we went to gather our little one. The drive seemed to take forever, but finally we turned into their driveway. Only three puppies remained. One was our Scarlett.

"Where is she, Mom?"

"Uh, well, the white line on her hip is there... and she's bigger...but she looks a little different, huh?"

Oh, my word! She had broken out in a full-blown case of Springer spots! Our Scarlett had freckles that marched up her legs, across her back, circled her tummy and sprinkled her tiny face. Spots or not, we agreed Rhett would love her anyway.

We were not disappointed when we arrived home. Rhett was always happy to greet us, but that day there was something special going on. He could sense it and so could we. From the moment he laid eyes on her, he was smitten. He sniffed at her, licked the last splashes of milk from her ears and face. He kept glancing up at us as if to say, *Wow! Thanks a lot, guys!*

As the months passed, Rhett and Scarlett became inseparable. There was no taking one to the store, to the vet or for a walk without the other. She would chase him relentlessly, not slowing down until she had a firm grip on one of his long curly ears. She teased him by taking his toys and tugged at his favorite blanket. He countered with a series of fake menacing growls. She wanted whatever he had. Gentleman that he was, he pretended it didn't matter. He would get up and walk away.

"He may be a gentleman," I told a girlfriend one afternoon. "But he's more wimpy Ashley at times than the determined Rhett." We chuckled at the thought of their not-so-subtle differences.

In time it was apparent that this little girl was no angel and no lady either. Like her namesake, she was one determined competitor. And it continued well into her next years. She'd catch a ball in mid-air intended for Rhett, grab a sturdy stick found after a morning storm, or a frog that Rhett had spotted, and claim it as hers. She stopped at nothing. When scolded, she would merely shake her stubby docked tail so hard, her whole body would vibrate. Our laughter only encouraged her.

"Miss Scarrrrlett, do fries come with that shake?" our son would ask in his most Southern drawl. And we'd laugh even more. One afternoon I was watching them run around the backyard. Scarlett was up to her normal antics. But this time she was jumping completely over Rhett's back and lunging at him.

"Look at that girl!" I mumbled to myself, shaking my head at her rowdy behavior. She was moving further and further away from being a lady with every sunrise. *Would she ever become the lady I'd hoped for?*

Scarlett's visit to the groomer's that week could not have come at a better time. Her debutante appearance was long overdue. She emerged from the groomer as a vision of beauty and grace. Nothing but the best for her. High hopes abounded. When we picked her up, we were not disappointed. Her nails were neatly trimmed and painted with Kiss Me Pink gloss to match her new sequined collar. A pink bow clipped to her neatly combed ears punctuated her femininity.

She sat poised in the van. I slid the side door open, and she stepped out as if a starlet's slippers had touched the red carpet. She pranced into the house, peering first to the left, then toward the back door, looking for her beau.

Rhett was lounging contently under the Newport tree, near a cluster of Lady Banks roses, when he saw her. *Or was it her?* Something was different. He sat up, staring in her direction.

Scarlett stood radiant and graceful. She glanced over at Rhett, contemplating her next move. She waited, then waited a smidgen longer before gently gliding off the stoop and onto the grass, hesitating with each step.

Rhett stood, planted his paws, and barked once. Her smooth, calculated motion exploded into an intense gallop in his direction. But Rhett, privy to her escapades, was too fast for her. He leapt forward, doing a 180 in mid-air, leaving her rolling in his dust!

The prissy pink bows were the first to go. She didn't even notice. Making a mad dash for Rhett, her manicured nails dug into the grass and the sandy soil.

"Oh, no!" I groaned, watching them make their rounds along the fence line. "SCARLETT, NO, NO! COME!"

After several attempts to catch up to one another, racing back and forth, they ran toward me with my firm *Come!* command. Their tongues dangling, they panted in utter exhaustion at my feet. Rhett had a twinkle in his eye that said he'd been waiting for this moment. It was pay-back time! And he enjoyed every second.

Scarlett looked as if she'd been rolled in whole-wheat flour. And those Kiss Me Pink nails were like an auto mechanic's. The sequined pink collar had lost some of its glitter, too. Her body quivered with excitement. I knew right then she had no memory of her grand entrance only moments before. My hopes of her becoming a charming lady had vanished amid the well-trimmed roses and azaleas.

Later that year, while I lounged on the screen porch, Scarlett snuggled next to me. My rocking chair made a soft creak. She lifted her head. Rhett didn't budge. She had no desire to wake him. She was no longer the rowdy tomboy on a rampage to make his life miserable. No amount of nail gloss, grooming or buttons and bows would do it either. Plain and simple. She had grown into a bit of a lady. For now anyway. It had just taken time. *And isn't it just like Scarlett to do it her way, in her own sweet time?* I tickled her behind the ears and winked. "After all, tomorrow is another day. Right girl?"

The Far Side

Gretchen Nickel

Linda O'Rourke

Whereafter

Elizabeth Robin

he strokes my back the way he did just before
he'd fold me in his warmth. scalp tingling,
i sit on the stump of a ponderosa pine,
the sky as cerulean as the ocean we swam
on our honeymoon. i hear the waves
through the trees, lapping some magic shore.
i crouch, hunched and small under that blue.
i sense his fingers flutter through my hair,
smell that vanilla musk, wonder: tree bark?
his skin? and tears dampen dry tinder.

the wind sways the treetops
not our island shore. a breeze
touches me the way he did.
i watch the pinetops and calm.

where green meets blue
i remember, he loved that view
stitched into the seam
of this whereafter
memories seep through

Sandy Dimke

Yesterday's Gone

~

James A, Mallory

I checked my math twice after I got the call. Yes, it has been forty-three years since we first walked the halls of a dormitory called Bigelow on Western Michigan University's campus. We often had little more than lint in our pockets back then, yet that September our biggest worry was what to wear to our first Icebreaker—the big party of the new semester.

You stood out during our years in college. And not just because of your trendy sideburns that matched your full afro. You had a mystique. It likely grew out of a combination of your quietness, calmness, and your accumulation of martial arts belts.

We partied a lot over the next few years, but that diminished as we found our grounding as students. We overcame our early bad grades and financial difficulties to find passions—writing for me, photography for you—that shaped our futures. You joined me at the student newspaper and shot the photos for the first magazine-type story that I published. We'd stepped onto our life paths—good friends, though not the best—by the time we had turned our tassels.

I was the first to get married. You took the photos. Wedding photography became a lifelong second job for you. We stayed in touch after graduation; celebrated a number of holidays with spouses and friends; and took at least one couples trip together.

You eventually returned to Detroit. I made a brief stop in the city, but Atlanta was my future.

We lost touch for a period of time, as we went about our careers and families. We only reconnected two years ago thanks to the persistence of your wife. She wrote me a letter, and told me of your recent health issues. I called you—man, it felt so good to catch up. Through the grace of God, last year we had a reunion with several others of the brothers of Bigelow at my sixtieth birthday lunch in Detroit.

We promise to stay in touch, as old, reacquainted friends are apt to do. But time is tricky. You look up and realize a year has passed without any contact. You hope everything is okay. How easy it would have been over the last twelve months to phone or send a text. I did neither.

Your wife called this morning. I absorb the news and tell my wife. We cry. I head to the beach; I need to process the news. Walking along the surf, I smile recalling those early and mid-years of the 1970s. Life has been good. But, the inevitable circle of life has closed ... much too soon ... for you.

Yes, yesterday is gone, but the memories remain. Rest in peace, Willie L. Lloyd.

On the Beach

Charles Harrison

On a beautiful Saturday morning in late May, Gordon had settled into his beach chair with his nose to his laptop and his cellphone to his ear, oblivious to his splendid surroundings. Dogs frolicked and chased tennis balls as pelicans dove for fish. Dolphins cruised and leapt, while beachgoers walked, biked, or sunbathed. Gordon, unaware, just worked.

Suddenly, something disturbed the birds, and a strange man approached. While Gordon was corpulent and florid, this mysterious creature was gaunt and pale with thinning white hair and the eyes of a zombie.

"Do you like coming to the beach?" the stranger asked in a raspy voice.

"I don't know," Gordon responded without looking up. "I've never been here before. My grandchildren have begged me to come, but I've always been too busy. I decided to bring my laptop and phone and give it a try."

"Are the kids enjoying themselves?"

"I guess so. I don't know where they went."

"Have you noticed the dolphins out there, or the pelicans?"

"I'm in the middle of something now. I'll look in a few minutes."

"It could be too late then."

Looking up for the first time, startled by the man's wraith-like appearance, Gordon inquired, "Say, who are you, anyway? If you are looking for a handout, forget it."

"My name is Theo. I work for Charon. He would have been here himself, but he can't tolerate sunlight."

"Who is Charon? That name sounds familiar. Have I met him?"

"No, you haven't met him. The first meeting with Charon is the final one."

"What's that supposed to mean? Where did you come from? I didn't see you approach."

"Where I came from doesn't matter, but where you are going does."

"You're talking weird. Did you forget your medications?" Gordon asked. Then he shrugged and refocused on his computer. "Go away. I need to get back to work."

"Before I leave, I have an important message for you," Theo said. "Charon will pick you up at your office this evening after dark for a short ferry ride."

The words *ferry ride* triggered Gordon's memory. Eyes now on Theo he said, "I have read all that hooey about being on the back nine and re-adjusting priorities before it's too late, and now you're telling me that I'm about to putt out on the final green?"

"I know nothing of golf, sir."

Gordon's gaze drifted out over the beach and the ocean, and for the first time, he noticed the serene splendor. A lone dolphin broke the surface. Gordon's eyes followed three pelicans skimming the water. Everyone on the beach seemed to be enjoying themselves, and he began to sense that perhaps he was missing out on something. Then a subtle smile creased his countenance. Gordon looked up at Theo and said, "Well, I have a message for your boss, Theo. No way! I am not going. Not only will I not be at my office this evening, but no other evenings as well. I have a few more holes to play and a chance to salvage this round." He closed his laptop, put away his phone and said, "I'm going to find the kids."

"You can say or do whatever, sir. But, once Charon has scheduled a ride, the passenger is not given a choice. Charon will pick you up this evening wherever you are. It is inevitable. So, you had best enjoy this, your first and final day at the beach."

And Theo was gone.

That evening during a late dinner, Gordon regaled his wife with the story of his encounter with Theo. After three martinis and half a bottle of vintage Bordeaux, he found it hilarious. He climaxed his narrative by looking up and shouting, "Look, Theo, wherever you are, I'm still alive!"

"I'm right here, sir," a raspy voice replied. "I'd like you to meet Charon." Beside the dining room door, discernible to Gordon only, stood the eerie figure of Theo next to a skeletal bearded specter with eyes of fire, holding a long pole in his right hand and emitting the foul stench of burning brimstone. Gordon's startled gasp and sharp intake of air lodged a chunk of prime beef in his trachea and he couldn't breathe. His distress prompted furious but futile action by his wife. She screamed for the cook to call 911 and pounded on Gordon's back yelling at him to breathe (they didn't teach the Heimlich maneuver in modeling school). Gordon's gaze, at first defiant then desperate and pleading, fixed on Charon. Charon and Theo ignored him as they waited patiently for the end. To them, a few more minutes out of many millennia were insignificant.

The wail of an approaching siren disturbed the tranquility of the neighborhood. Soon afterward came the rhythmic, barely audible sound, perhaps just imagined, of soft ripples rolling onto the banks of a river.

The Trip up the Hill

Phil Lindsey

He climbs the steps slowly, for he's an old man.
There's a bench at the top of the hill.
He sits, and he rests, and he listens,
but for the birds, the air is quite still.
He searches for life on the hillside.
The pheasant and foxes are gone.
But it's springtime, and flowers are blooming,
and the deer and the squirrels carry on.

He closes his eyes, reminiscing,
when they lay on the grass by the tree.
A butterfly floats past her tombstone;
it's not the living he came here to see.
There's a bittersweet patch on the hillside,
and he makes a bouquet for her grave.
He places it softly beside her,
then descends, with barely a wave.

There's a lifetime of love in his actions.
Now, eternity calls out his name.
Their earth-life together was Heaven;
without her it isn't the same.
So mourn not for the departed.
Save your prayers for those living alone.
Request that God grant them safe journey,
on their trip, up the hill, to His home.

Whose Ghost Is Here

Ann Lilly

I always knew the house at 333 Kingsway Drive was haunted, but in the ten years we lived there, I had never been afraid. We were the fourth family to live in the house and as far as I know, no one died there. I assumed it was a friendly ghost, or at least one that liked us. Built in the 1930s, the house had its share of creaks and groans that I attributed to settling, but a few things happened that defied explanation.

The first thing we noticed was the closet door in the first floor bedroom. It was always open. The bedroom floor sloped a little, causing the door to swing open, so we had to push really hard and listen for the latch to click to keep it closed. I can't tell you how many times I found the door wide open after being positive I'd shut it tight.

Then there was the light in the basement—an old porcelain socket with a naked bulb, mounted overhead on a floor joist. It had a metal pull chain, but it was also connected to a wall switch. The light was always on. The light bulb looked ancient… small, yellowed with age, and completely frozen into the socket. The bulb burned for ten years and, for all I know, may be burning still.

For a long time I blamed it on our kids. They played in the finished side of the basement and only ventured to the other side by request, to bring something upstairs or to shift laundry from the washer to the dryer. They said it was creepy over there, especially the big gas furnace with octopus arms. In the winter, my husband returned from work after dark. Driving down our driveway, he'd notice the light shining in the basement window well, and he'd tell the kids they'd left it on again. Then one of them would run downstairs and turn it off.

After living in the house for several years, we realized the light had a mind of its own. It was always on. My husband was convinced there was a logical explanation. He replaced the wall switch, checked the breaker and made numerous attempts to remove the bulb. He'd turn off the light, and within a few hours it was back on.

But the fun really began when we put the house on the market. My husband was the one pushing to sell the house and move to Hilton Head Island; I was reluctant to leave Lexington. One evening, when home alone, he was locking up before going upstairs for the night. He locked the French door in the dining room, and when he stepped back, something poked his foot from under the floor. He said it felt and sounded like someone in the basement hit the floor directly under his foot with a broom handle. He shrugged it off to old house settling. He took another step back and was poked under his other foot. The hair on his neck bristled, and he said, "Hello, anybody here?" He stepped and bounced all over that floor trying to make it pop again.

Now any normal person who has ever watched a scary movie would have enough sense to get the hell out of there. But no, not my husband. What does he do? He goes into the basement! And, the light was on. He'd spent the past ten years renovating the house and knew every inch of it. He was certain he would figure out what happened but could find nothing wrong. I thought maybe the ghost was mad at him.

Several months went by, the house was under contract, and we were getting ready to move to Hilton Head Island. In the middle of the night I woke up to our teenage daughter shaking me out of a deep sleep. She was upset and kept saying, "Something poked me."

Once she calmed down, she told us she'd been watching TV in the family room and had fallen asleep on the floor. She woke up when something poked her from under the floor. She first thought she had been dreaming, but then it happened again. My husband checked the basement to find nothing out of place, but of course, the light was on. Our daughter camped on our bedroom floor for a week until we moved.

I've often wondered if the new people had any ghostly activity. Sometimes when we visit friends and family in Lexington, I get sentimental and ride by to see the old house. The last time was at night, and I stopped and looked down the driveway to the basement window.

The light was on.

Donna Varner

Island Writers' Network

Rachelle Jeffery

102

Blue Magic

Thelma Naylor

As Captain Willy eases the bow of the *Reef Hugger* toward a buoy designated for dive boats, I lean over the rail of the sun deck, face into the wind, and close my eyes. The warmth of the Caribbean washes over me while the sea air erodes the tensions of civilization. Our dive group will spend a week on this state-of-the-art liveaboard which accommodates twenty scuba divers and ten crew. *An entire week of collecting watery tales to take home,* I muse.

It's 8:00 a.m. The dive deck is abuzz with activity, frenzied really, as everyone gears up for the first dive of the day. Two at a time, I bound down the steps from the sun deck to the dive deck and join my buddy at the station where our equipment is stowed. My husband Bill and I were certified over twenty years ago and have been dive buddies ever since. Safety, above all, was instilled in us right from the start so as we gear up, we check each component like a pilot checks his plane before entering the cockpit. The briefing is about to begin.

Emilio, the local dive master, stands glistening in his native sun. His dark body taut yet limber, his Rastafarian tresses neatly coiled under a colorful cap. His gestures, fluid and rhythmic, synchronize perfectly with his voice, a mellow mix of sounds from several continents. Song-like, his words transport me to the kingdom below.

"This dive site be called *Blue Magic,*" he begins, raising his eyebrows to emphasize the word *magic.* "The island people tell all kinda tales 'bout this place." He grins, and continues describing the site in a matter-of-fact way, pointing to a whiteboard where a childlike drawing outlines the reef below. "On the reef, we see turtle, barracuda, angelfish, lovely sea fans. We go no more than ninety feet deep, but look beyond, maybe two-hundred feet down, and you see eerie shapes. Those be parts of wrecks. This be a deep dive, so no longer than forty-five minutes."

Following the dive briefing, Bill and I double check each other's equipment, mentally going down our list—*computer activated, air on and flowing through regulator hose and mouthpiece, mask clear, fins secure?* Following this intense scrutiny, we look at each other through our masks and make the OK sign, joining the tip of the thumb to the tip of the index finger. Feeling hot and clunky in tightfitting wetsuits, carrying a forty pound tank, wearing fins that force a duck-like walk, we're anxious for the comfort of the water.

Emilio and the dive staff assist each diver with entering the water. When my turn comes, Emilio intones, "You ready ma'am?" With much relief, I nod, yes. Then, in dive lingo, he chants, "Giant stride off the side, go!" I waddle to the side of the boat, launch myself into the very best *grand jeté* I can muster, and with a splash, pierce the cool water. Like a submarine exhaling, I gently sink—down, down, down, right into the center of *Blue Magic*.

Bill and I, and four other divers, are in Emilio's group. At sixty feet, we adjust our buoyancy to neutral—going neither up nor down—and wait for him to join us. He finally comes down and like well-mannered fish, we let him lead us through the mysteries of the deep.

In the safety of the group and with a knowledgeable local in the lead, I can finally relax and really start my dive. I'm where I want to be—immersed in water, so soothing, so quiet. I'm suspended in a liquid space, weightless, just drifting along. All sounds are muted. I hear only the muffled roar of the ocean and my breathing through the mouthpiece—rhythmic, yoga-like, breathe in, exhale, breathe in, exhale… I watch the air bubbles rise, mesmerized. Sunbeams shatter the surface and spotlight the corals, the fish, and in shallow areas, make the sand twinkle like a disco floor. In the hazy distance, I watch a majestic eagle ray glide by.

I'm now *one* with the water. My regulator hose transforms into flowy hair, the wetsuit into a sequin sheath narrowing to a point, the flippers fuse into a powerful tail fin flaring out at the end. *I'm a mermaid!* I revel in the magical swish of that tail, the fluid movement of a sea creature gliding through the chaos of the oceans. I sashay through the corals, whoosh past sea fans waving in the current, and slalom through giant blades of kelp swaying to and fro like bamboo sways in the wind. A manta ray swims by, and I tail fin frantically to keep up with it, so engrossed, that I forget about my buddy.

From deep below, a glow catches my eye, distracting me from the chase. I detect shadowy figures weaving in and out of eerie structures, geometric cubes, rectangles, triangles, scattered over the ocean floor like a set of children's building blocks. Then I remember, *Those must be the pieces of the wrecks.* The human-like silhouettes beckon me to join them. Intrigued, I start down. A gradual darkening changes the colors, pink turns to purple, orange to brown, and further down still, everything turns gray. A sudden drop in temperature gives me chills as I enter this dark, mysterious zone. I'm inexorably drawn toward the friendly silhouettes as by some otherworldly force. I sense a kinship with them. I'm so close now; I reach out to touch hands with the nearest one who is coming up toward me.

Beep, beep, beep! My dive computer startles me. *Was I dreaming? It seems I just got here, and it's time to leave already?* I check the display. *Oops, I've exceeded the recommended dive time, I've sunk to one-hundred ten feet, and yes, it's time to go back to the surface. Fortunately I still have plenty of air.* Waving goodbye to the silhouettes, I look around for my dive buddy, and for Emilio. *Where are they? Where's the boat? I'm lost… Panic…*

No! I'm trained for this, I know what to do. *Breathe, count to ten, regain my composure.* I stabilize at my current depth, neither descending nor ascending, and staying vertical in the water, do a 360 to make sure the others aren't behind me. I watch my air bubbles float upward like sparkly dots, and see the sunlight shining through the water. As I look up, Bill's bright green fins come into view, no more than ten feet above me. Like bells tolling in a distant field, I hear the clanging of his knife against his tank and realize he's trying to get my attention, motioning me to ascend toward him. I begin my ascent, reaching Bill after a few seconds, and we both continue upward together, hoping the boat will be nearby when we reach the surface. To avoid decompression sickness, or *the bends*, the ascent must be controlled, no faster than one foot per second, and include a three-minute safety stop fifteen feet from the surface. I watch the depth gauge continually so as not to rise too fast. Arriving at the fifteen-foot point with plenty of air, I settle into perfect balance for the three anxious minutes remaining. I muse about what just happened. *Did I experience nitrogen narcosis, raptures of the deep, the Martini effect? Scary!*

One minute into our safety stop, I hear the muffled chortle of a dinghy motor, and a splash brings Emilio down to us. He signals, asking if we're okay and whether we need more air. "I'm OK," I signal back. Bill does the same. Two more minutes of safety stop. Emilio stays facing us and keeps our attention on him, knowing that divers in panic can become irrational. Those two minutes last an hour, but finally, we can complete the ascent, and the three of us rise together for the last few feet.

As my head breaks the surface, I'm relieved to see Captain Willy steering the dinghy with the other four divers in it. The Captain immediately reassures us with, "No worries." It turns out that we hadn't drifted that far away and that the crew had had our bubbles in sight the whole time. These folks are experienced and know how to deal with recreational divers.

Back on the *Reef Hugger*, I cross the dive deck to my designated spot, and there's the sun, the vastness of the ocean, and a bonus—a warm towel and a just-baked chocolate chip cookie, tenderly brought to me by my buddy.

Relaxing before dinner in the dreamy light of dusk, I prompt, "Emilio, tell us the tale of *Blue Magic*." Needing no further encouragement, he points toward the tip of the island closest to us and begins.

"In Thalo Bay, that village there, people say the wrecks of *Blue*

Magic be haunted. Water *duppies*—local ghosts—be livin' there, spirits of lost souls from the ships." Dramatic pause. "But they be good *duppies.* One day, the fishermen go fishin', but after many hours, come back with only seaweed in the nets. Next day, they come to the harbor to go fishin' again and, like magic, find the nets already full of fish." Another pause. "That be a good *duppy* deed, they say."

Laughter, applause, dinner bell! *Yes, there will be plenty more fun stories like this one during the week.*

As Captain Willy starts the engine of the *Reef Hugger* for the overnight trip to the next dive site, I rush to the stern to watch the wake and the foam whipped up by the engine. Leaning over the back rail, salt water splashing up at me, hair blowing around my face, I fixate on the hazy aura over *Blue Magic.*

"That's where I almost became a *duppy*," I murmur.

A Maze

Elizabeth Robin

i walked the labyrinth today
after staring at cathedral ceilings

they say it mimics the twists and turns
life offers. but its stones are smooth
the path clear, each curve mapped

no choices
no disasters
no tears

just the mild joy
of a childish meander

persist, and find
life's center

a mythical cliche
a fenced limbo
tied to dust and ashes

as in many paths
everyone arrives

Tango-19

John MacIlroy

The sky went black, as black as the stealthy double hull of *Tango-19*, on this, her last mission.

Commander Meredith Conrad eased the ship over the lip of the small planet, one of a cluster now called The Outer Rim. After her sixteen years in space, she had yet to get over the sheer terror of Deep Space Darkness. The human spirit—she now knew this for certain—needs to see *something* in the night sky.

Meredith was, at least technically, still mostly human. So she let linger the memory of those brilliant night skies that once held nothing but wonder and promise—until the day the skies of Earth forever turned angry, and the rains began.

Of the ships launched before contact with Earth was lost, fewer than forty made it to the three cluster planets. No one knows why so many ships simply disappeared, or why three weeks ago things started to go wrong on Outer Two, the smallest of the colonies.

"Maybe it's the Darkness," she remembered the Command Admiral saying just hours ago. "Nothing really like it. Does something to the soul. Crushes it, really, particularly in the older refugees. They simply give up. It's the trace of some primal fear the night monster under the bed, something in the dark woods. It's in us all, somewhere." He seemed to pause just then, an unusual tic in his command-crisp style. "But maybe you're lucky, Commander. You volunteered to be one of the early Augments, and the first to receive the neural-chip implant. That seems to be the ticket, something in the procedure that hardens your soul, toughens you up. Likely a tender mercy, out here. You never talk about it, and this is your—what—ninth mission?"

"Yes, sir. Number nine." *But, she thought, you are so terribly wrong about my hardened soul.*

"Easy mission profile tonight, Commander. A class-alpha replenishment. Called them a milk run, back when we had real milk, you know. Max load. Mostly habitat modules, water pods, tons of freeze-dried stuff. You'll be dropping enough to keep our people down there on Outer Two for the next ten years."

The Admiral smiled.

"We're also loading a dozen of those virtual reality pods. Even put a few movies in their programs. Picked them out myself. Hollywood classics, mostly funny stuff. Maybe help them settle down."

The movies, she guessed, were likely from his own collection, a quirky link to his own past. The Command Admiral had been stationed on Outer Two in the early years, and always took a special, and generous, interest in missions to that planet.

"I'm authorizing a full crew, with sub-orbital drop. You'll be driving one of the newer ships, *Tango-19*, with the advanced hyper-drive. But you won't come close to unleashing that on this trip, although she's programmed for a full wormhole punch next month. Even Consortium doesn't know how far she can go. Just keep the tiger in the cage tonight, Commander. No stupid stuff."

"Aye, Admiral. *No stupid stuff.*"

A little loose, she knew, but something Command Admiral Marcus "Bull" Conrad would let slide from his only daughter, along with the mere hint of the hug that followed. He always made sure no one was around to see this shared breach of regulations, a surprisingly tender lapse by the crusty, no-nonsense Admiral and the daughter he loved. But he had been too old for augmentation, and his soul ran deep indeed.

As she left to begin her pre-flight, Commander Meredith Conrad prayed he would understand. *Someday.*

★ ★ ★

Her crew talked about it all the time. Not another Augment among them, they were a young lot, eighteen men and seventeen women, and ship's company was the only family they knew. At first she dismissed it all as the stuff of dreams, idle chat of the young in the endless blackness of space. Talk of another universe, a rip in space bathed in the glow of a New Beginning of Time, out there somewhere—anywhere—away from the Darkness.

Even if beyond their imaginations, it was not, she could see, beyond their hopes.

She came to marvel at their full humanity and their yearning, and she soon understood what she had to do.

In the end, it was an act not only of faith and hope, but of love.

"No, father," she whispered in the soft green glow of the flight deck, her fingers dancing across the flight controls as she sequenced the fusion hyper-drive, the ship quick to respond with an awakening shudder, as if it too understood its destiny. "How very wrong you are, as I now know only too well the full-throated cry of the human soul, the irresistible pull of hope and things unseen beyond the dark horizon..."

★ ★ ★

Under the soft pink of a late afternoon sky, with the gentle sounds of New Eden a living testament to the depth of her soul, Meredith Conrad was lowered into the ground, just four days before her eighty-sixth birthday. She would now rest under the monument that had been built in tribute to the crew of "The 19," as people now called them, the pioneers who found their new universe and seeded this new world, a planet remarkably like the Earth. But an Earth yet unspoiled, and forever bathed in a gentle glow from the two suns around which it orbited.

She had borne no children, quiet talk of problems in the augmentation process. That point, however, was now moot. Her young crew had been prolific, giving them all a future. And hope.

The monument itself was built from a section of the *Tango-19* navigation grid, its glass polished and embedded in a black, marble-like base. As her casket fell below the rim of the soft soil, the glass caught the light of the two suns, just right.

It was a joyful burst of color, a magic prism of hope and faith, the Darkness, if not Death, overcome.

Peace

Anatol Zukerman

So quiet – I hear a big moon
climbing the frozen sky,
humming his golden tune.

Hemlocks stand to attention.
Maples don't even try
to shiver.

A somnolent river
flows waste to a somber ocean
under the star-studded dome.

Soldiers who came back home
sleep under crosses and rocks
smiling with lipless teeth.

Peace, brothers, peace!

Native Americans, Salem witches,
highway drivers and teenage killers,
mafia bosses, disgruntled workers
all of them sleep till dawn.

Only a distant moan
of a train or God at a black horizon
whimpers away like a child.

Cumulous clouds glide
without a sound or shift.

This night is a generous gift
to all who try to forget
how lucky one must get
to live on top of this hill
without killing or being killed.

A Look Inside

Lindsay Pettinicchi

Marilyn Lorenz

The Boys

Marilyn Lorenz

I was six years old the first time I heard them. They were twelve, on the stinky, smelly boy edge of adolescence. Typical of boys that age, they ran and jumped for no reason whatsoever, pelted each other with anything available, climbed garage roofs and hit baseballs to the end of the street. They planned and schemed, ate unwashed Concord grapes growing wild behind someone's house, wore the same muddy shorts two days in a row, and began to sing. It was the singing that made them bearable. Otherwise, I might not have paid any attention to them at all, even though one of them was my brother Bill, and the other his best friend, Bud, a nickname for Edward.

In 1943, World War II was in full operation, so in between their flagrant shenanigans the boys sang "Coming In On A Wing and a Prayer," "Mareseatoatsanddoeseatoats" and "Chickory-chickchallah,challah" or "You are my Sunshine." As their voices started to change, it was hit or miss on the notes most of the time, but they laughed and sang anyway. Whenever I heard them, I hid nearby so they couldn't see me. There was probably nothing in the whole wide world I wanted more than to sing with them, but they scorned girls openly, particularly younger sisters.

In the summer of 1944 our family bought a farm on the Eastern Shore of Maryland. It took seven hours to drive there in our old '41 Chrysler with no air conditioning and a slobbering dog. My father smoked, so the ashes flew back through his open window. Between the ashes, the slobbering dog, my brother and his baby alligator from Florida, and car sickness, things didn't go well. Potato chips sometimes helped with the nausea, but what helped most was singing! Sometimes after he gave me careful instruction, my brother would let me sing melody to his emerging harmony. Amazingly, my nausea would go away until he tired of the effort. But I was thrilled to think that sometimes, whatever I had was enough. When our summer at the farm ended, we went back to our home in Montclair, New Jersey, and my brother and his pal Bud took off again for places girls didn't know about or weren't allowed.

Somewhere between 1945 and 1947, everything changed. Most of the older brothers who had been serving in the military came home, and the boys I idolized began following them around, listening to their stories, and gearing up for manhood. Girls started to creep into their conversations. Girls, old cars, state championships, and all the stuff teenagers talked about back then. My brother and Bud disappeared into the world of high school without a single backward glance.

My friends started begging to come home with me.

"Why my house?" I'd ask.

"Why not your house?"

My mother DID make the best cookies, but that clearly wasn't why they wanted to come home with me. Nope. My brother had somehow turned into a Greek God, and even ten-year-old girls knew what that looked like. So all of us hung out at my house between bike rides, checking to see if by some miracle, Bill and his friends were there. Fat chance. We were lucky to see them at football games in the fall talking to cheerleaders in their letter jackets, or at the track in the spring, lined up watching Bill throw his lengthening frame over high jumps. That is, until Boogie-woogie rolled onto the scene.

Boogie-woogie fit my brother's charismatic personality like a perfectly tailored sport coat. Our beautiful mahogany grand piano leapt off the floor in the living room, pounded painfully into action by fingers insistently seeking louder and louder interpretations of whatever piece he chose. Everyone in the neighborhood knew when Bill was home. Everyone. Even in the dead of winter, Boogie-woogie passed through storm windows and doors, floating on the frigid air with uncharted exuberance. There was no end to it. Albert Ammons and Meade Lux Lewis took up permanent residence in our living room. Even my friends got tired of waiting for Bill to finish playing Boogie-woogie so they could ogle him standing up. And frankly I couldn't wait for the phase to pass, so Bud and Bill would get back to singing. Well, actually, I don't think they ever stopped singing, but they did more of it out of the house. Every once in a while though, particularly in summer, I'd hear them on the back porch of our house in Montclair, or walking up a field at our farm in Maryland harmonizing to "Nero My Dog has Fleas," which they will surely go to Hell for because they changed the words to "Nearer My God To Thee." Bud always sang the harmony in a confident and serious tenor. Bill's job in the duo was to carry the melody line energetically forward, all the while smiling and engaging whatever audience they accumulated along the way, and sometimes throwing in a flippant bass note he couldn't resist.

There was palpable magic in their sound.

That time in our nation's history was heartrendingly strong, innocently epitomized by boys like Bud and Bill, who grew up at the feet of men whose heroic and youthful optimism won World War II. Neighborhoods and families in places like our town carried the promise of peace forward together. It was like a collective sigh of gratitude settled on us all, and stood us up smiling and determined. To say that it was a magical decade to grow up in America would be to vastly understate its power.

But getting back to my boys, Bud and Bill developed an astounding repertoire of songs to harmonize to during the last years of high school. Songs like "Got Along Without You Before I Met You," "Coney Island Baby," "Roll a Silver Dollar," "Frankie and Johnny," "Flaming Mamie She's a Sure Fire Gal" and many more, delighted small crowds of sighing teenaged girls at the slightest opportunity. My mother would stop making dinner and stand leaning on the kitchen counter to listen to "A Man without a Woman," rendered hopefully by her hungry son and his friend. They could really sing now. Confidently, happily, exchanging the harmony part back and forth. Even my father, who was a very hard man to impress, raised his martini in surprised salute to their sound.

It wasn't as if Bud and Bill couldn't do anything else. They learned to sail on Chesapeake Bay estuaries and Maine's Lake Webb. They danced with their girlfriends even when everyone was watching. They went down to the "shore" leaning out the windows of old cars, pretty rich girls laughing and tossing crumbs in their direction. They worked at Bragg's haberdashery, and sold Christmas trees in Bond's parking lot. They mowed lawns, bought "white bucks," took SAT's, made applications to East coast colleges, and waited to see who would take them in. All of this while I was still in grammar school, saluting the flag with a hand over my heart. In September 1949, they left for colleges hundreds of miles apart, and our house was a lonely place.

Six years between siblings is a very large gap, brought on, I suppose, by the fact that we were born during the "Great Depression." But I had at least caught a glimpse of what it was like to have a brother, albeit briefly, and missed his presence every day that he was away at college. Thanksgivings and Christmases became precious beyond dreams, every day filled with Bill and Bud, new college songs they taught us around the piano, new friends in and out of the house, parties frosted with the magic of fulfilled expectation. My mother was the heart of our family, but Bill was the sun, moon and stars. And Bud, as I grew, became the man I wanted to marry.

It's probably quite common for younger sisters to covet their older brother's friends. After all, they, like fathers, are the first exposure we have to the mysterious opposite sex. But always when I asked my brother if he thought I could marry Bud someday, he would answer, "Sis, you're twelve years old (or fourteen or sixteen) for God's sake, Bud has girlfriends his own age. He will probably be married before you even get home from college!" And then would follow the forty-four reasons Bud would never be interested in me. That didn't do much for my confidence at the time, but somebody has to tell you the truth, and very often that truth came sailing straight at me from my brother.

In the 50s the boys finished college, joined the Navy, got married, left the Navy, had children and moved away to start their careers. Every so often they would see each other at mom's house over a holiday, or after a wedding or funeral in town. It was rare then to hear them sing and made the occasions when they did all the more precious. In their sound was still the golden beauty of warm summer days, walking in new snow toward our house in the streetlight of a winter evening, decorated Christmas trees next to our piano, all of childhood well lived and loved.

And then, incredibly, it was thirty years before I heard them sing again. Thirty years of births and deaths, sunshine and shadow, successes and failures, all of it played against turbulent decades of social and personal change. The seventies, eighties and nineties put every child born in the thirties to the test. Learn and change or become irrelevant, learn and change or be left behind. So learn we did and change we did, and kept going.

I lost my first husband to a heart attack when I was fifty. After eleven years of widowhood, I brought a man I admired and loved to meet my brother and his wife at their second home in Tortola. It was no surprise to me that Bud also had a second home in Tortola, as the boys had kept their friendship alive through all the years of working, raising families, long distance sharing, and even one divorce. One night Bud invited us all to dinner, held in a flower filled courtyard in his home. It was such an emotional experience for me I could barely carry on a conversation. There they were, those same old boys, the same sea-salt kissed hair, the same crinkling blue eyes, the same smiles, the same laughter. Sometime between dinner and dessert, I found the courage to ask them to sing one song for me. At first they demurred, claiming they didn't really sing much anymore. But I persisted, knowing there would never be another chance like this one. They relented, and I closed my eyes. I don't remember the song they chose out of the many they knew, but I do remember thinking that the magic in their sound was as simple as love. Love and trust, love and life, love. I don't suppose I will ever hear music that will move me more.

When I'm on my way to heaven, if the boys have made it there first, I'm going to listen all the way up the beams of light to St. Peter's gate. If I'm lucky, through the gate will float the gentle harmony of them singing "Nearer My God to Thee," and St. Pete will have forgiven the boys for changing the words. If I'm not lucky, I'll hear Boogie-woogie, and heaven won't be nearly as much fun.

Legacy

~

Suzanne Eisinger

"Tell me the one about Uncle John and the hayloft," I remember asking. The wide bristles of the wire brush slipped easily—too easily—through my grandmother's thinning hair, so I switched to the comb that lay on the kitchen table beside us.

"You know that story better than I do," Grandma laughed shortly. She leaned back against the kitchen chair, a bath towel draped around her shoulders and closed her eyes contentedly as I continued to comb her hair. She had absolute trust in me, though she had no reason to. It was the first time I had ever given anyone a haircut and, other than the few glimpses I had bothered to give the beautician when she cut my own hair, I hadn't a clue how to perform the procedure myself.

She didn't care, though. "Just take off enough so it doesn't show under my wig," Grandma had instructed. The wig in question lay in a small heap on the other side of the table, its usual resting place unless company came to the door. Then, she would quickly sweep it up and tuck it over her own locks, grown progressively sparser since the radiation therapy months earlier.

I stood nervously behind her, perched up on tip toes so I could get a better view of the crown of her head. The first cut was the hardest. I pulled up a length of hair with the comb and, after a lingering moment of hesitation, snipped off what seemed like an inch of pale gray hair. I took a deep breath, feeling almost winded by the accomplishment, although Grandma's eyes remained closed. *Ok,* I decided. *I can do this.* So, I pulled up a second swath and then another, lower lip bitten in concentration, until I'd finished the job.

"All done," I announced and only then did I realize that she had remained quiet for the entire haircut.

"Hey, you didn't keep your end of the bargain," I scolded her.

Grandma smiled drowsily. "How do I look?"

"Beautiful," I answered. "But you owe me a story."

"Ok," she agreed. "Keep combing, though"

Grandma settled into her chair, her eyes open but now focused on a time over sixty years ago. "It was autumn and my brothers and sisters and I were helping out with the harvest. This was way before those big combines that all the farmers have nowadays. Back then, you harvested by hand. So, while our Dad drove the horse and wagon, we walked alongside and picked the corn and threw it into the wagon as fast as we could.

"Eventually, it started to get dark and Dad drove the horse at a faster pace. We were already pretty tired and this made it harder to keep up. Well, I guess my brother John had had enough. I looked up just in time to see an ear of corn sail past me and hit Dad in the back of the head. I suppose it could have just been a bad toss, but I doubt it. John had the best aim of all my brothers."

Her hair, mostly dried now, curled up at the edges as I gently combed through it. It was wispy, like a baby's, and seemed almost as fragile as my grandmother did these days. I glanced down at her cheek, a jaundiced yellow in color, and tried to believe that it didn't mean anything serious. Out in public, when she caught people glancing, Grandma would comment playfully on what a great tan she had. People always laughed at the joke, relieved that they could sidestep the painful truth of the matter.

"Now, our Dad had a temper," she nodded soberly as she spoke. "And he pulled that horse up, twisted around in the wagon and demanded to know who had done it. John straightened up and said it was him—didn't even try to say it was an accident. He was almost as big as Dad now and wasn't afraid of him anymore. Well, Dad swung out of the wagon fast and walked up to John, slapping him hard in the face. Told him he'd finish the harvest himself and then ordered the rest of us to go back home. We didn't want to, but we left John behind in the field. He was there for hours, finishing the last few rows by himself.

"The next morning, John wasn't in his bed. We looked around the house for him, calling his name, but he didn't answer. We were headed out to the fields when all of a sudden we heard this howl of anger like I had never heard before. It was Dad's voice, and it was coming from the barn."

Grandma paused, a distant smile on her face. She was right there, seeing everything again in her mind's eye. "Turns out, John spent the night in the hayloft. But, I guess before he left the barn, he decided to leave a little present for Dad. He collected some manure from the horses and hauled it up to the loft which was at the top of a ladder and behind a little door that swung down from a hinge. To get the hay you'd just climb up, swing open the door above your head, reach in and pull down the hay, usually without looking where you were reaching. Why would you? All that was up there was hay." She chuckled. "Except that morning, when Dad reached up, he got a handful of something he wasn't expecting, and as he pulled his hand away, the whole mess of it fell down on top of him.

"I don't think I've ever seen Dad that mad in my life. Oh, he was a sight, I can tell you. It's a good thing John was nowhere to be found, because Dad had grabbed the pitchfork on the way out and looked like he was ready to use it. But John was halfway across the county by that time and didn't come back for two days. Can't remember what happened to him then, but I don't think he regretted it one bit."

I smiled. She was right. At age sixteen, I knew that story by heart, but there was nothing like watching Grandma tell it. I handed her the mirror, so she could judge for herself the success of my first haircut. She nodded in approval, rewarding me with a wink. I smiled in proud relief.

★ ★ ★

The lunch rush had ended by the time we arrived at the restaurant, only a few scattered customers remained. Grandma, sporting her new walker, and I, my new driver's license, walked in slowly, our steps in sync, until we found a booth closest to the entrance. In all her years, Grandma never learned to drive, preferring to rely on family members to take her where she needed to go. Today, she relied on me, and I took the responsibility seriously.

I watched as she took small sips of her soup, the spoon shaking in her hand. We both pretended not to notice, distracting ourselves with idle conversation. Yet, as the meal neared its end, I found myself not wanting to leave. It was too soon, I thought, though I didn't exactly know why. So, I talked her into having a cup of coffee to keep the connection going a little longer.

I half-filled her coffee mug from the white carafe, hoping this might keep it safe from her trembling grip. Grandma held the mug in her hands, bending her face into the curls of steam that escaped. She closed her eyes, her face peaceful.

I took advantage of the silence. "Tell me a story," I asked, my teenage voice plaintive like a child's.

"Baby girl, you know all my stories," came her reflexive reply.

"Tell me about Mama and the rooster."

Grandma chuckled. "Oh, that one." She took a breath before continuing.

"When your mother was young, we raised chickens for extra money. Most of the hens and roosters roamed freely around the house. They barely looked up when one of us would walk by. But, there was this one rooster that was just plain mean. He chased anyone that got too close. Well, your aunts were older and didn't pay him much notice, but your mother was terrified of him. And he knew it. So, every day after school, as she walked down the lane toward the house, that rooster would chase her and peck at her legs and ankles until she made it inside the door."

She took a sip of her coffee. "This went on day after day for weeks. Your mother would carry on and beg me for help, but I told her she needed to stand up to that thing or it would never leave her alone.

"One day I watched for her after school and, sure enough, that rooster was watching, too. As soon as she got within a few yards of the house, that thing charged her from the bushes. Your mother screamed and began to run for the door. And I knew right then that she wasn't going to stand up to that little devil. So, I walked over, grabbed it by the neck and carried it to the butcher block in the barn. That was the end of that. Problem solved."

My laughter echoed throughout the restaurant. I had heard that story from my mother, too. Even after all these years, she recalled the feeling of horrified amazement at how her mother could chop off the head of that rooster without a second thought.

Grandma and I returned to a companionable silence before I asked, "Tell me about when you quit school."

She eyed me for a moment with a guarded expression. Grandma was the matriarch of our family in every way—strong, proud, and fiercely protective of those she loved. But, she wasn't proud of leaving school early, or the limited opportunities she'd faced in life because of it.

She sighed. "Back when I was growing up, there weren't any school buses or carpools. Kids had to find their own way to school and, in the country, those schools were few and far between. Our farm was a long way from town, so the closest school to us was seven miles away. For as long as I can remember, my brothers, sisters and I would pile into the wagon and drive the horse an hour to school every morning. That was after we finished our morning chores. If we woke up late, we'd have to walk, which meant two hours instead of just one and the teacher would punish us for being tardy.

"By the time I was fourteen, I had had enough of getting up before dawn and coming home at dusk. Between the chores and the homework, I barely had a minute to myself before it was time for bed. Most of my siblings had already quit or graduated, so it was just me with my two younger brothers.

"One night, I told my parents that I wouldn't be going to school any more. My mother was more upset than my father—I suppose he figured I would likely end up as a farmer's wife anyway, so what was the big deal? Best to have me on the farm learning how to run one properly. But, my mother wanted me to graduate. When she couldn't change my mind, she sent a message for the schoolmaster. The next afternoon, he came to the house and demanded that I return to school. But, I stood my ground and said it was my right to decide when I had had enough. So, the schoolmaster left and I worked my family's farm until I got married. And then I worked my own farm."

There was more to the story, but she would never tell it. Over the years, I learned from family how she had endured years of abuse from her husband. How she had finally left him—unheard of in those days—preferring the scorn of her neighbors to one more day of living in fear. How she struggled to support her three daughters by working menial jobs.

It was her strength and tenacity that pulled her through. Even now, as her frail body began to slump against the booth cushions, her resolve was unmistakable. "Don't you *ever* quit school, you hear me?" she ordered, gripping my hand as she did so. "You make something of yourself."

"I will, Grandma."

★　★　★

Over thirty years and a thousand miles separate me from those afternoons with her. Verdant fields of corn replaced by miles of sandy beaches. Spring has returned to Hilton Head Island. The predictable wave of tourists is still weeks away, so our family has the beach almost to ourselves. It is a time to savor.

My sons are up ahead, throwing a football back and forth. I smile as I watch them try to outdo each other. Lagging behind, I walk with my daughter, her long, curly hair windblown by the ocean breezes. Reflexively, I reach up and comb my fingers through her hair but barely make it an inch before the first tangle stops me. Grandma's comb would never have had a chance with this child. Neither would scissors, since she is fiercely determined to grow her hair until it touches her ankles.

Still, as we inch toward the spreading waves, gasping with surprise when the cold hits our feet, I am struck by the many ways these two women I love and have loved are alike. Strong and stubborn, sharp yet loving, my little girl is very much her great grandmother's kin.

"Tell me a story, Mom," she asks, her arm swinging with mine in a wide arc. "Tell me about your grandma."

I nod. "Which story do you want to hear?" I ask, for she knows every one there is to tell.

"Tell me the one about your Uncle John and the hayloft." She giggles, already thinking of the ending. It is one of her favorites.

"Ok, but I get to comb your hair," I bargain with her. It is a constant struggle between us—a mother's quest for order versus a child's blissful chaos of tangles.

She agrees and plops down on the sand, pulling me down with her. I wrap my legs around her from behind and softly pull my fingers through her thick, amazingly alive curls.

Life goes on. Through her stories, my grandmother's legacy touches a new generation.

The Kite

Phil Lindsey

Dad made a kite out of paper and wood,
and a white, ripped up sheet for a tail.
We all watched with wonder when without any wind
he could make his kite rise up and sail!
The trick, he would tell us, is to run just a bit,
then let the string play out just so.
There is wind up above us that you cannot see;
it will make the kite rise up and go.

Up went his kite, high up over the trees,
and soon it was dancing with clouds.
It dipped, skipped and twirled as he tightened his rein.
"It's MAGIC!" we shouted out loud!
The kite, he would tell us, responds to your touch.
Don't hold it too loose or too tight.
Be forgiving, yet firm, let it fly by itself,
and most times it will turn out all right.

Dad gave the kite to the youngest child there,
and the rest of us waited our turn.
The kite soared, then collapsed; our confidence too.
Dad taught; we attempted to learn.
Life, he would tell, us is like flying a kite,
You hold on but you cannot control.
Don't let a failure or lack of success
stop you from reaching your goal.

Be like the kite; reach as high as you can.
Set your goals high, and dance with the clouds!
But remember and honor the wind you can't see.
It's your faith that will make others proud.
Faith, he would tell us, is the courage to fly,
and belief in a presence unseen.
But most of all faith is the strength to go on,
when your kite gets stuck high in a tree.

Once Blackbirds Flew

Marilyn Lorenz

There's a ribbon of road 'round a spool of a hill,
in a basket of yellow-green pines,
where stitched fences run, by wheat rip'ning in sun,
under patches of blue denim sky.
And a little old farm, with a little old barn,
near a house made of love that was mine.

When I close my eyes tight, sometimes late in the night,
I can dream it as if I were there,
and I think I can see, in that girl that was me,
something straight, and strong, and fine.
But then when I wake to a new dawn and sky,
every day in a life going by,
I fear what is left of the girl that was me,
is this one unshed tear in my eye.

Dancing With a Sleeping Man

Jim Riggs

Karla Stevens tapped her black, patent-leather shoes to the rhythm. Her slender, runner's body moving to the music. The band played their version of Cher's hit song, "Believe." Karla listened to the music, sitting alone at the round table in the ballroom, sipping a glass of Riesling.

She watched a couple of dozen teachers bouncing and swaying on the little dance floor. She shook her head, thinking, *Here I am in Louisville, at the convention of the National Education Association watching everybody else having fun. I need a dance partner.*

Her dark eyes scanned the room, looking for an available man. Every male she saw was either dancing, sitting at a table holding hands with some woman, or covered with tattoos and wearing a nose ring. Then Karla glimpsed three chairs pushed together on the far side of the room. A man wearing jeans, a dark-tan sport coat, and a turtleneck lay across three chairs. His hands pillowed his head.

Carrying her glass of wine, Karla glided across the ballroom. Her tall, thin figure swaying to the tune.

Karla viewed closed eyes behind stylish bronze metal glasses, heard even breathing, and admired a strong face and a burly body. He was tall and athletic-looking. *I'm five foot ten. He's definitely taller. That's good. I wonder if he likes a willowy woman.*

I shouldn't wake him; the man must be tired. Maybe I'll just sit and gaze at him. She smiled at her brash humor. Karla pulled up a chair. When it squeaked across the floor, the man opened his eyes.

Pretty eyes, she thought. *Baby blue like the northern sky at sunset.*

"Hi," he smiled.

"Hi."

He stared at the beautiful face. *Her dark eyes are intense,* he thought. *Does the angelic face mean I've died and gone to heaven?* He scanned dark eyebrows, long black lashes, heavy black eyeliner, and perfect bright red lips. *An angel would not have lipstick.* He smiled. "Hi, beautiful woman. Are you a dream or can I touch you?"

Without waiting for permission, he reached out his hand and touched a round cheek with a finger.

A shy smile flashed across his face. "You're alive. That's a good thing."

"Sorry to wake you," Karla chuckled. The man held out his hand. She reached to meet it. He surprised her with a fingers up grip that he used to pull himself to a sitting position.

Stronger than she looks, he thought.

"I was asleep. Sorry."

"I'm sorry," she repeated. "I'm sorry, I woke you,"

He read her name tag out loud. "Karla Stevens. New York."

"Dan Stewart," he said. "When you marry me you won't have to change your suitcases."

"My suitcases?"

"The ones with the initials *KS* on them."

Karla beamed and held out her left hand, showing Dan her ring.

"See this?"

"You picked a man with vision."

"You have a strange sense of humor. The ring means I'm married."

"Then why were you coming over to me, waking me up? Asking me to dance?"

"I didn't ask you to dance."

"You were about to."

"What makes you say that?"

"You left the dance floor. You pulled up a chair in front of a sleeping man. You either planned to ask me to dance or to marry you. Missed the ring. Maybe you have an unhappy marriage. Maybe you're looking for a new man."

"You are crazy, Dan Stewart. I think I made a mistake. You are a crazy man."

"So what are you doing here?"

"I needed somebody to dance with me. Look around. All the rest of the guys are hooked up. Then I saw you. I wanted to dance. You weren't hooked up, so I thought I'd ask you to dance with me."

"I was your last chance."

Dan received a frown for that joke. "No commitment. We'll just dance and get acquainted."

"You aren't going to ask me to marry you?"

"Definitely not. I don't know you, Dan Stewart. I just want to dance with you."

"Marriage later? After you learn how charming I can be?"

"Marriage never! I'm happily married."

"Does your husband know you ask strange men to dance?"

"You're not strange. You're a relatively nice looking man. You're wearing shoes without socks. That's strange. Do you dance?"

"In South Carolina, stylish guys wear deck shoes without socks. As far as dancing, it isn't my strong suit. I do pretty well slow dancing. I could try to follow if they're playing some bouncy thing like 'I Believe.' You want to risk it?"

"Works for me. Come on."

She grabbed his hand, leading him onto the dance floor.

They played another fast rock song....

Dan seemed to follow her moves fairly well, like a dog in training.

Then the band played Foreigner's, "I Want To Know What Love Is."

Dan asked, "Ok. Fast or slow? Seems in-between."

"Look around. Most people are dancing close together."

Dan nodded. Karla put her hands around his neck. He grasped her slender waist with both hands feeling the open lace and knit patchwork of her long black dress, pulling her close; moving his feet just enough to be able to say he was dancing. Karla's body melted against him, following his lead. Dan let his hands drift to her slim hips.

Karla thought, *I like the feel of this man. And I like the feel of his hands on my hips. I'm glad I woke him.*

"Are you cold in that dress? It has some open spaces."

"That's to make it look alluring. Sexy is one of the words used in the description in the catalog."

"You better not ask for your money back. They told it like it is."

Dan reached up and ran his hand through her long black hair, following it to her shoulders.

"I love your hair. The color of a raven. Do you mind if I touch it?"

"You already did. But no. I like your touch."

He moved his hand back to her narrow waist, gently pulling her close again.

"Tell me about yourself," he said, his mouth nearly touching her ear. "I assume you are a teacher, since this is a teacher's convention. New York City?"

"Smithtown. It's on Long Island. I teach fifth grade. And you?"

"I teach high school science in Bluffton. That's in South Carolina. Pretty easy compared to teaching fifth grade."

"Are you a native?"

"Of Bluffton? Hardly. No one is a native of Bluffton."

"How about South Carolina?"

"Born and raised right here in Louisville, Miss Karla. Tell me about New York."

"You know New York. We have one of the largest cities in the world. Let me tell you about Smithtown." She leaned her head back and smiled.

"You have a beautiful smile. Your fifth grade boys must be in love with you."

"Thank you, Dan. Pay attention. I was teaching you a lesson about Smithtown."

"Sorry, Ms. Stevens. Go ahead."

"Smithtown is on Long Island, almost fifty miles from the Empire State Building.

"We have a statue. Whisper the Bull. The city basically stole it from the artist; commissioned it, never paid for it, and got it for a pittance after he died. Now, he's our most famous resident."

"You must be ashamed to live in Smithtown."

"I'm proud of our town, Dan."

"Who's the sculptor? The guy must have been perturbed when you didn't pay him for his work."

"Charles Cary Rumsey. The man should have been paid. I'm a little ashamed of our political powers."

"I may have to go to Smithtown and see Whisper."

Karla frowned. "Maybe not."

"Are you ashamed of me?"

"You might be hard to explain to my husband."

Dan smiled. "Just kidding. Another joke. Sorry."

"How about South Carolina? What's special about Bluffton?"

"Salt Marshes. The Inland Waterway. Alligators. Wading birds. Oyster beds. Shrimp. Tourists. We're the gateway to Hilton Head Island. We have two outlet malls."

"Sounds like a beautiful place. Do you kayak on your salt marshes?"

"I do. Do you kayak?"

"On wild rivers. I love white water."

"Do you have one of those little skirt things?"

"I do."

"The ones you wrap around you to keep you dry when you roll?"

"They work. Do you do rolls? Do you flip upside down?

"Not much of that kind of water in the Lowcountry. We have the ACE Basin. If we plan it right, we can paddle downstream on the out-flowing tide, mess around a while, and then paddle back downstream to our starting point on the in-flowing tide."

"We? Are you inviting me?"

"You're happily married."

She pulled him closer and looked away. "I lied about the happy part."

"In that case, let's paddle Ebenezer Creek. It's in Georgia; runs through a marvelous cypress forest. The trees are southern ballerinas at their first ball, big whoop dresses with, what do you call them? Crinolines inside? The cypress trees have huge knees that are tall and black, like giant spears used by the knights. If you like to kayak, I'd love to share the black water of Ebenezer Creek with a beautiful woman. We could paddle down to the Savannah River, eat lunch, and paddle back up Ebenezer Creek to our starting point."

"My marriage is becoming shaky, Dan Stewart. Keep talking, I might take you up on your offer, Mr. Dan."

The music had gained speed. Other dancers were attempting to match the beat. Karla and Dan stayed at the edge of the dance floor, clutching each other close, hardly moving their feet. A big burly guy bumped Dan.

"Excuse me," the guy apologized.

Dan smiled at the man. "No, my fault. I was standing right in your way."

He led Karla to a table. Sitting, he kept control of her hand with both of his. She added her other hand on top.

He looked at her hand. "You have long, lovely fingers." Then he moved his gaze over her body, up to her eyes. *And you have the body of a lovely woman,* he thought. "I must be careful here, Miss Karla. I don't know you very well, but I'm liking you a lot. Our time together is fleeting. Soon, Louisville will be gone, you'll be only a beautiful memory. Do we stay and dance and talk and enjoy our time or what?"

Karla returned his gaze, looking at his blue eyes, swallowing a deep breath. "Why don't you walk me to my room and then catch the shuttle bus back to wherever the South Carolina delegation is staying. Maybe we can have lunch tomorrow."

"You're telling me to slow down?"

Ignoring his question, Karla clutched his left hand and led

Dan toward the exit. In the elevator, at the third floor, he took her in his arms and kissed her. At the seventeenth floor, the door opened and he stuck his foot in the opening.

"Somebody might need a ride." She pushed him through the door.

In front of her door, Dan kissed her again, their mouths exploring, learning. And then he kissed her again and again.

Finally, Karla placed her forearms on his chest. Drawing a deep breath. "Noon at the north entrance, by the huge bust of Thomas Jefferson." She stretched up on her toes, touching his lips with hers.

"I'll be there," he promised.

She reached up with her hand, caressed his cheek, then turned into her room, leaving him alone in the hall.

As Dan walked away, he glanced at his watch. It was just after two in the morning.

Dan was fitful. He was almost asleep when his roommate walked in an hour later. He rolled over facing the wall. Sleep continued to elude him. He lay awake, thinking of Karla, remembering her touch. *I think I love her,* he thought. *How can I love her? She's married. Maybe I'd better not show up for lunch.*

He took a deep breath and slept.

In the morning, Dan scanned each person he passed in the mammoth auditorium, searching for a graceful women with raven hair.

Conference speakers talked of educational techniques, teacher advocacy, and political action. Dan's mind overflowed with a tall, slender, sinewy woman, a woman who had reached out and grabbed his heart as if it was an October leaf, fluttering from a maple tree. At 11:50 a.m., Dan rubbed his hand over the letters of a Thomas Jefferson quote below the bust of our third president. He moved his fingers over the words: *Honesty is the first chapter in the book of wisdom.*

At noon he glanced at his watch, walking a circle around the statue. Ten minutes later, he made the trip again. Finally, he gave up and went looking for the New York delegation.

He found a man who seemed to be in charge. "I'm looking for a teacher from Smithtown, New York. Her name is Karla. Karla Stevens."

"I'll check the roster." He reached for a notebook. Then immediately, turned back toward Dan. "Wait a minute. I remember. She was feeling ill. She took a taxi to the airport and flew home early this morning. Sorry."

Dan walked past the South Carolina delegation, climbing to an empty section of bleachers, high in the upper deck. Resting his elbows on his knees, his head in his hands, he attempted to focus on the stage far below. His vision of the stage and of the speaker was blurred. Another image dominated his mind, a graceful woman, a woman in a tight black open-knit dress, dark hair curling around her shoulders. He raised his fingers, touching his lips.

Then Dan leaned back, sprawling in the lonely seat, in the empty row, in the empty section, contemplating what to do with an empty heart.

Security Questions

Bill Newby

My file drawers weren't working.
Rollers were jammed, and I couldn't find my key.

I had placed my trust in safe choices –
my maternal grandfather's first name,
the street where we lived when I was born,
the school where I finished first grade.

Then, on a recorded call
"to improve customer service,"
after my name, social security number and address,
I couldn't remember an answer.

It's worse than moving,
leaving an old neighborhood,
having to find new friends, stores and restaurants.

Discovering the new is easy.
But the old slips out of memory
without a word of goodbye.

And when we try to summon it,
we're shocked by how bare
our room has become.

Linda O'Rourke

The School Bus Driver

Marty Ferris

Alone on the school bus parked just off the lane, 63-year-old Catherine Simmons eased her ample frame down—deep, into the driver's worn leather seat. *Lord, just for a minute, let me rest my weary eyes,* she silently prayed.

A bit later, the gray-haired bus driver reached over, flipped a switch to open the doors, and let the fresh afternoon air sweep inside.

Today, the school year ended. Minutes ago, with a heavy heart, Catherine watched the last child, Sarah Williams, a second-grader, leave the bus, take her father's hand and start walking toward their veterinary clinic.

From the beginning, and for her entire first-grade year, "Good morning, ma'am," were the only words Sarah ever volunteered. After that, she walked to the back of the bus and sat alone. Catherine often thought, *what a sad, little life she leads.*

That morning, as she got on board first, Catherine asked, "Sarah, how are you today?" Before moving to the back of the bus, the child responded, "I'm fine, ma'am." One at a time, at all the other stops, children got on and happily greeted each other. The bus driver thought, *how sad, they all have friends but nobody is paying any attention to Sarah.*

Catherine loved her riders. Each school day, trudging onto the bus, they greeted her with clean, soap-smelling faces and a cheerful, "Good morning, Miss Catherine, ma'am."

But this year, when the children returned after Christmas vacation, something new and exciting happened. Something that affected the children on her bus—especially little Sarah.

Shaking her tired head, Catherine repeated, "What a year this has been, what a year this has been." Her head drooped and her eyes closed. Miss Catherine, Hilton Head Elementary's Route

141

#43 driver for more than 20 years, sat on her bus; letting sweet breezes sift through the open doors and lull her aching body. Lightly dozing, Catherine's mind wandered back to the first school day after the Christmas holidays. _

In January, little Andy jumped aboard, in a rush to tell her all about it. *Andy is always racing to get on the bus to go home, but not so much for getting on in the morning,* Catherine noted.

Wide-eyed with excitement, Andy said, "Today, we got three new kids, Miss Catherine, and they are going to be on our bus today. Just think, coming from so far away to be here with us in South Carolina."

"Oh, my stars, child, where are they coming from?"

"I can't remember it," Andy replied, trying hard to think. "But, my teacher says it is far away."

"Well, don't you worry none, principal Taylor already told me."

Earlier that afternoon, Ruby Taylor had called Catherine into the principal's office. She handed her the names of three new students, all boys, and their address for pick-up and drop-off. The principal said, "The Vidal family is from Madrid, Spain, and their father, Luis, a well-known architect, is working on a special project in Atlanta. The children and their mother will only be here until the end of the school year. Although the children have traveled to many places, this is their first visit to the South. Please, make them feel welcome. They boys are in second, third and fourth grades."

At the time, Caroline thought, *three little boys from Spain, living on Hilton Head Island, South Carolina and they will be riding on my bus—imagine that.*

As school let out, Catherine stood watching her Route #43 riders file out of class. After hugs and greetings, her regulars jumped on board. Tall for their ages, the three Spanish boys waited beside the bus.

"Hello there," Catherine said. "Are y'all coming with me?" Silence. Stepping forward, the tallest boy, politely offered his hand to Catherine and said, "Good afternoon, I am Javier Vidal, and these are my younger brothers, Pablo and Marco." Caroline shook Javier's hand, and smiled at his brothers. "Well now, let's get you boys on board, and we'll all head home. Sit wherever you find a space."

The bus driver did her 55-minute afternoon run; dropping the regulars off at their appointed stops. She thought, *I'm right on time, just four children left; in the front, the three Spanish boys and in the back, little Sarah.* In her rear-view mirror, she noticed the little girl watching the boys.

Catherine knew the location of the little, yellow house the Vidal family had rented for six months. Back from the road, it sat among huge magnolia trees, and in the middle of a wide expanse of green lawn. A long, gravel, driveway stretched down to a dusty, unpaved lane. She turned the bus off Highway 278, drove slowly down the lane, and stopped at the end of their driveway.

Before opening the doors, she turned to Javier. "Who is coming for you?" He pointed to a blue Subaru. Over her shoulder, Catherine saw a slender woman, with shoulder-length brown hair, step out of the car and wave.

"Ella está aquí. Vamanos." Javier spoke rapidly in Spanish while helping his brothers gather their back packs. Then, they all moved to the door. "Careful," the bus driver warned, as she followed them out.

"Y'all get off slowly, now."

"Good afternoon," said the young woman while embracing each of her boys. She spoke to them in Spanish before saying, "Thank you for bringing my sons home. I hope they have not caused any trouble."

"No, ma'am," the driver said, shaking her head. "I'm happy to oblige. My name is Catherine Simmons, and, Mrs. Vidal, your boys will be safe riding with me."

"Thank you, and please—call me Patricia. My boys seem to like the school. We hope to have a wonderful time here."

Catherine laughed, "Of course, you will. Good night, now."

As the doors closed, she could hear the youngest, Marco, call out, "Buenas noches, señora."

After that, every school day morning, Patricia Vidal—slender, with chestnut-brown, almond-shaped eyes—stood next to her boys and waited for the school bus to roll up. If the bus arrived late; Patricia waited with them. Each afternoon, she was there— ready to greet her children. On rainy mornings, they stood huddled together under a colorful, over-sized umbrella.

That first afternoon, Catherine noticed Sarah walk to the front of the bus as the Spanish boys were leaving. Flattening her little face up against the front window, she stared at the family outside.

Alarmed, the bus driver spoke out, "Child, what are you doing? Sit down, so I can start the bus, and get you home." Without a word, Sarah walked back to her seat.

At Sarah's mailbox, Caroline came to a stop, put the bus in neutral, and turned off the motor. Nobody was waiting. Cheerfully, she said, "Here we are. Can you tell me good night?" The child responded, "Good night, ma'am." The bus driver watched as the little girl began walking up to the clinic. _

The second morning, Marco got on the bus and looked back at Sarah. Glancing up through the rear-view mirror, the bus driver saw him walk back and sit next to her. Sarah seemed indifferent, which didn't surprise Catherine, who shook her head, thinking, *that child never speaks to anyone.* Oddly, Sarah did speak to him, but her eyes remained transfixed on the figure of Marco's mother fading in the distance as the bus drove away.

Sarah and Marco were deep in conversation when other students got on. Same thing on the ride home. As the little boy got up to leave, Sarah slid up from her seat to walk behind him. With her face glued to the window, she watched as Patricia bent down to kiss her youngest son. Sarah stared as Marco hugged his mother. "How was school today?" Patricia asked while smoothing down his hair and lightly kissing his cheek. Seeing Sarah standing, Caroline spoke firmly, "Child, sit back down."

The next day, when he got on the bus, Marco smiled and

said, "Move over Sarah, I want to sit with you." After that, they were inseparable. As the days moved along, other children began sitting closer to them. Eventually, through her rear-view mirror, Catherine could watch Sarah and Marco surrounded by a circle of children, all giggling in hushed tones.

What is happening here? Caroline wondered. *I know Sarah suffered in first grade. All year, she could hardly wait to get off my bus and run back to the animals at her father's veterinary clinic*

Catherine had established a rapport with many teachers at the school during her 20 years as a bus driver, so she visited Sarah's second grade teacher, and asked, "Are you noticing any changes in the child this year? Agnes Riviera laughed happily. She gestured for Catherine to move closer. "Indeed, we all do. Isn't it exciting? Sarah laughs and plays with the other children now. I think the little Spanish boy is a positive influence. They sit next to each other and work on little projects."

Well I'm not surprised, thought Catherine.

Agnes continued, "You know, he told me last week, his name is Mark, not Marco and, for me to please remember to call him by his American name."

"What are you going to do?"

"Call him Mark, of course."

"Catherine, you remember last year, Sarah was never a problem. But, we all worried. Playing by herself at recess, and at lunch, eating alone; she seemed so lonely. We watched as she shared lunch with the birds hovering around the school grounds. Other than that, she just slipped in and out of class without a word."

"Yes, last year, it seemed that Sarah's life began after school."

Agnes said, "She is the only child in my class with no mother or grandmother."

Caroline nodded, "I thought that might be the case."

At that moment, fourth-grade teacher, Elizabeth March, stepped into the break-room. Gesturing to her, Agnes said, "Elizabeth. I am explaining to Miss Catherine about the wonderful change in Sarah. She wonders what might be the cause."

Elizabeth March taught twenty-three children, and had very

few unpleasant things to say about any of them. "Well, if you are asking, let me tell you what I see." Her praise of Javier, the oldest, caught Catherine's interest.

"Javier is so intelligent. He works well at the computer, and loves reading about South Carolina history. The other day, he asked me if his class might have a field trip to Rose Hill. I said we would try later his year. Perhaps his mother might like to help organize it?"

Agnes urged, "Ask her, right away." Catherine listened as Elizabeth continued. "Javier is also an exceptional soccer player. Already, he is organizing my fourth-graders into teams. His brother, Mark, wants Sarah to play. So, she is on the team, as well.

Elizabeth looked at Agnes. "Sarah is quite the tomboy"

Agnes, said, "Catherine, getting back to Sarah, why not check with Margaret Carson, Pablo's teacher?

Walking back to the parking lot, the bus driver saw Sarah with Lucy and Andrea, two little second-grade-girls jumping rope together. *What a difference*, Catherine mused.

Just before class the following day, a smiling Catherine knocked on the door of Margaret Carson's third -grade room. Long-time friends, the two women had been singing together for years in the soprano section of the Presbyterian Church choir.

"Welcome Catherine," Margaret said cheerfully. "I am delighted to have you visit."

"Thank you, " said Catherine. "You know that the Spanish boys are on my bus."

Margaret nodded. "I believe it. Something good is happening in their house. They are always polite. The brothers are very close. Javier is protective of his bothers. Pablo is cordial, and artistic. He is always busy creating beautiful projects."

Principal Taylor entered the room. After listening for a minute, she nodded in agreement. "Yes, all three Spanish boys are special, but it is little Mark who charms everyone. Always smiling, that little one makes friends quickly."

In February, Lucy approached the bus driver. "Valentine's Day is coming pretty soon, will you visit our class party?" Catherine laughed, "Of course, I will be pleased to be there."

The day of the party, Dr. Jake, Sarah's dad, brought a small brown and white puppy and one kitten for Show and Tell. Sarah stood in front of the class, explaining how to care for the animals, while Mark walked around the room holding them for the children to pet. Catherine smiled thinking, *I know Jake loves his little girl. But, not since her mother died, have I seen Sarah this happy.*

A bit later Mark walked over to Dr. Jake and said, "I told my Pappi in Atlanta about Sarah. He is happy my best friend is the daughter of a veterinarian." Jake threw back his head and laughed.

At the party, Catherine sat next to the second-grade teacher. Several children rushed up. "We love you, so, we made valentine cards." Catherine hugged them and accepted a basket filled with home-made cards and tasty, chocolate-chip cookies. She watched Sarah go over to Patricia and tug at her sleeve. Smiling, Patricia bent down to accept a valentine card. "Thank you, my dear," she said, while gently stroking Sarah's hair. For a moment, the little girl's eyes sparkled with happiness. Even though she enjoyed playing with Mark and his brothers, Catherine kept noticing that Sarah tried to stand close to Patricia.

By St. Patrick's Day, the Spanish boys were behaving just like the rest of Catherine's family of riders. "Andy, Thomas, Javier, what's that soccer ball doing flying through the air on my bus? Don't let me see it again," she scolded. "Y'all going to behave like this on the field trip to Honey Horn tomorrow?" After hushed whispers and laughs, a humble Andy spoke. "No ma'am. Sorry, it won't happen again."

As the bus reached their stop, Mark said, "Tomorrow my mother is bringing fruit for everyone." Javier quickly spoke, "Is there a special fruit you would like, Miss Catherine?" Smiling, she answered, "Anything your mother brings me will be fine."

At Honey Horn, Javier and Pablo took pictures. Rushing to hand his mother folders, Mark said, "para la llamada." Patricia explained to Catherine, "Once a week, the children phone their grandparents, Javier and Aurora Rojas, who live in Madrid. Tomorrow, when we call home, Mark will share with them everything he learned today."

Caught in a sudden rain shower, the children jumped on board the bus. Catherine helped them dry off. Sarah quickly sat down and let Mark's mother rub her hair dry with a soft towel. With eyes half-closed, Sarah breathed in the sweet smell of Patricia's shampoo. Catherine noticed her look up at Patricia with an expression of complete adoration.

A week later, ready to take the students home, Catherine checked her list of riders. Four missing. She stood up and walked the bus. *Mark, Sarah, Lucy and Andrea. I brought them this morning. Where are they?* After a fifteen-minute search, a teacher found the missing group—sitting on the floor of the second-grade reading circle with Mark showing his friends pictures of the Alhambra in Spain. Gathering together the four children, the teacher marched them to the bus.

Catherine stood waiting. Looking directly at Mark, she said, "Children, you will never do this again; we all leave school together, and on time."

The real turning point came when Dr. Jake confirmed with Principal Taylor, "Sarah will get off the bus with the Vidal boys on Friday nights, and I will pick her up later." From that Friday on, Catherine dropped the three boys and Sarah off together and watched as a smiling Patricia welcomed them.

Once, Jake and Sarah picked up the Spanish family for a day of kayaking on Broad Creek. Another week-end, they went into Sea Pines and to Monarch Beach. Jake, Sarah and the boys splashed and ran through the gentle surf while Patricia watched them from under a giant, beach umbrella. Then, Jake, Javier and Pablo caught the Trolley over to Harbour Town to rent bikes. At sunset, they all climbed up to the top of the lighthouse.

This happy circle of activities with Sarah and the Vidal boys continued. In April, Mark asked his mother to invite the second-graders to their yellow house for a party. "Of course. We will include all the children—and Catherine," she said.

On Saturday morning before Easter, as Catherine drove into the Wal-Mart parking lot, she saw the Spanish family coming out of the store. Patricia stood beside the car as her boys took the groceries from the cart and loaded the back of the Subaru.

The bus driver thought, *the Vidal family has made this year something wonderful, but, school will end soon. What will happen when they leave us? What will happen to Sarah?*

In mid-May, a few teachers noticed their students were not talking as much about summer trips and vacations. Least of all the children who rode on Route #43. Andy asked, "Is it true Miss Catherine, when school is out, the Spanish boys will be leaving forever?"

"That's what Miss Taylor said."

Already, Mark had told everyone on the bus, "We meet Pappi in Atlanta, the first week of June, then, we go to New York. After that, we travel to the island of Majorca for our vacation."

Sarah asked, "What will you do there?"

"Swim and sail our boats. Javier and Pablo are good sailors, and they are teaching me. We will not go home to Madrid until school starts again."

"Gosh," said Andrea, "you guys are lucky to travel so much. Your family must be super rich." Javier and Pablo moved to sit near Sarah. "If you give us your address, we will help Mark write to you. You can write back, and tell him about all the animals you and your dad help at the clinic."

On the last bus ride, the Vidal boys signed their soccer ball. While standing, Javier whistled sharply, then, tossed his ball up in the air, all the way to the back of the bus. Andy leaped to catch it. "For next year," he yelled.

Then, one by one, the children left, and Sarah sat alone—again

At the last stop, Catherine got off and greeted Sarah's waiting father. "Well, school is out and the Spanish boys are gone. They are lucky to have such a wonderful life."

Sarah stood near her father, and under her breath whispered, "Yes, the boys are lucky, but not because they travel so much and have lots of fun." In a barely-audible, sad voice, Sarah continued,

"Javier, Pablo and Mark are lucky because they have a mother—who loves them."

Catherine's eyes opened wide while listening to Sarah's words. She glanced at Jake. Did he hear his daughter? Yes. His reaction let Catherine know he had heard. Jake's shoulders sagged; his face went white.

Then, the moment passed and it was over. Jake reached out and took his daughter's hand. Together they walked up the incline toward the clinic. They had animals waiting.

Catherine understood. It wasn't only Mark and his brothers, it was their mother, Patricia, who had captured little Sarah's heart.

Bang, bang, bang! "Miss Catherine, wake up. Are you all right?" UPS driver Harry Simms's loud banging on the bus window brought Catherine around. She jumped, wide-awake.

"Oh, my stars, of course, just closed my eyes for a bit." She was thinking, *I must get over and see Jake and Sarah tomorrow.* Catherine stepped out of the bus to show Harry she was feeling just fine.

After a quick visit, she waved, stepped back in, and started the bus. Standing next to his truck, Harry watched Miss Catherine's yellow school bus rumble down the road toward the highway.

Her 98ᵗʰ Birthday

Jeanie Silletti

We assemble every October
both for sibling friendship and delight in her elder years.
Dad departed from our circle decades ago
but remains a constant in our lives.

Out-of-towners have made their way to Carolina.
All are present for the Saturday honorary luncheon.
The fashionista enters adorned by a fuchsia fascinator,
a complement to the crimson walker by her side.

Escorted to a reserved seat at a long, ample table,
she greets her seven children and their spouses.
Healthy fare is served, a carrot cake her only splurge.
Blowing out the candles, we share her unspoken thought.

Heartfelt toasts and good cheer animate the room
until a silent pause and a beloved ritual begins.
At the first notes of a favorite song, "What a Wonderful World,"
she rises to slow dance with each of her four sons.

Cradled in their arms, she beams with maternal pride.
Wet eyes spread contagiously among the sisters.
A brother's piano medley softens our closing moments.
Amid farewells, we ponder her birthday wish.

DJ Murray

Medley Relay

Miho Kinnas

A moment after the starter buzz
spectators shout out streamers of cheers.
Five teams unreel in each roped waterway
their backstroke arms like masts hoisted for victory.

Eyeing for the timing, she slowly crouches.
Although swimmers always swim alone
a monarch on her shoulder keeps her company
appearing and disappearing as she pulls herself forward.

In the meantime another butterfly quivers
in the stomach of the next swimmer on deck.
After the first stroke with open arms
she no longer hesitates.

Every dive awakens the spine and stretches
the string of the relay for those who have gone
and those who will come to race one's heart out.
From here, the anchor embraces all the past journeys
and goes strong, strong, strong.

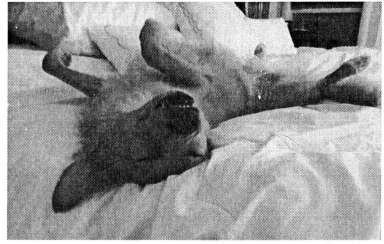

Terri Weiss

Hannah

Lisa Wilson

Hannah wakes me up at 3:00 a.m. to take her outside. Such a good dog. She does her business and walks the perimeter of the fence with Edward. Eating a couple bites of snow along the way, Hannah determines all is well in the back yard.

Since moving to Waterloo two years ago, it's been a while for the opportunity to see Hannah and even longer to have her spend the night. I often would dog sit Hannah and I have a special place in my heart for her. My own dogs, Lucy, Edward, Franklin, and Phoebe sniff Hannah over, their version of the welcoming committee.

Hannah is slowing down, as do most dogs at 14 years of age. I do see glimpses of a puppy as she gets excited to see me. She plays with tennis balls and chews on toys. But, she labors as she climbs the stairs, taking one at a time. I place her dog bed and blanket in my office because the room gets a lot of sunshine during the day and is cozy. There are no stairs for her to contend with.

As I head back to bed, Hannah decides to make her way upstairs. With some effort, she places her front legs on my bed and waits for me to lift her back legs as she doesn't have the strength to make the jump. She walks a couple of circles on the bed before lying down. Of course, her choice spot is pretty much in the middle. Lucy and Edward join Hannah in bed and that doesn't leave much room for Phoebe, Franklin, and myself.

Letting sleeping dogs lie, I decide to sleep in my recliner. Franklin and Phoebe will join me. I snuggle in with my fuzzy blanket and prayer shawl, and I only had one hot flash, thankfully. My cancer meds take my body from cold to hot so I prepare for the temperature swings. Franklin and Phoebe know the drill to jump down faster than I can toss off the blanket. A small price to pay for sitting on my lap.

I suppose some people will think I'm a bit odd, giving up my bed to a dog or two or five. Before bed last night, it occurs to me this may be the last time I see Hannah. It makes my heart ache and I think about how much time I have left and how many years cancer will rob from me. I can't entertain these thoughts for long as they overcome my mind with much sadness. Anxiety swirls within me as a hurricane of "what if" questions begin their torment: What if my cancer spreads? I can no longer work, I lose my house. But not tonight. Tonight, I enjoy my four-legged friends.

Before I settle in my chair, the big yellow lab stretches out with her head on my pillow. I hear her making a deep low moan as she presses her legs to push Lucy and Edward off the bed. Hannah slept like a queen, raising her head occasionally to make sure I'm still in my chair.

Life is short. Let your dog have the bed.

Late Saturday HORSE

Bill Newby

Phillip bounced the ball on the pavement—once, twice, three times. He already had H O, and Greg only had H. It was just a foul shot, but Greg had called, "No backboard," and that made it more difficult. Phillip felt a tightness grabbing his chest. A miss would drop him far behind, and he used each dribble to try to flush the tension away. Then he set his feet, brought the ball up so it rested in his right hand and launched it toward the rim. The arc seemed high enough, but the distance was a bit short. The ball fell, hit the rim's front edge, bounced back and dropped.

"R," Greg called as if giving news to the entire street. He grinned, walked across the drive with a broad-shouldered strut, picked up the ball and started dribbling around. Then he tried a mid-range jump shot. It missed, and Phillip ran to it before it rolled into the street. The driveway had room for two cars side by side, but it was only about thirty feet long before the sidewalk and the apron to the street. The street lamp across the street allowed some games to extend past twilight—a rare summer treat when nothing else was happening.

Phillip was relieved when his mother granted permission and Greg said he could come over. Much of the afternoon Phillip felt suffocated by his homework, reading the story about a man stuck in a snowstorm and finding answers for the Louisiana Purchase study guide. He still had to do the odd-numbered math problems and write a two-page essay. But for now, it was great having Greg there to help him escape.

Phillip dribbled up the drive and went to the right corner. He faced the basket. His feet were at the driveway's edge, almost into the bushes next to the path to the back door. From this angle he couldn't use the backboard.

"Try this!" The ball rose, fell, and kicked off the side of the rim.

Greg got the ball and tried and missed another jumper. Phillip went back to the corner. Once more he studied the near rim and tried to fly the ball smoothly over it. The ball dropped into the center with the sweet sound of rubber passing through rope.

"Swish!" Phillip shouted, ran to the ball and shot it to Greg.

"You didn't call it," Greg said and slowly walked to the corner, ball in hand, while he studied the rim.

"Come on. Back up," Phillip demanded. "My feet were all the way to the edge."

Greg inched back, took several dribbles, and missed.

"H O," Phillip declared. "Now you're in for it." He went to the base of the drive, near the sidewalk, and started dribbling toward the basket. "Lay up around the back." Phillip had been practicing this shot all summer after seeing Bob Cousy playing for the Boston Celtics. Cousy would race up the court as defenders tried to get in his way. Then he'd pass the ball behind his back to another Celtic or return it to his right hand and take his own shot. It was a smooth piece of acrobatic misdirection.

Two steps before the basket Phillip cupped the ball in his right hand, carried it around his right hip, and transferred it to his left hand. He completed the circle, across his belly, back into his right, and jumping off his left foot, he lifted the ball toward the backboard just to the right of the rim. The ball thumped off the plywood and dropped into the basket.

Phillip threw the ball to Greg. At the end of the driveway Greg practiced bringing the ball behind his back, but when he approached the basket to take his shot, he lost control and the ball rolled into Mr. Tippet's yard.

"R," Phillip said. "We're even." He ran down the small slope, across the grass. Mr. Tippet usually cut his own grass, but Phillip had done it twice during the summer when the Tippets had gone somewhere on vacation. It was a big yard and took a long time to cut.

Phillip thought, *how can I pressure him?* He went back to the base of the drive. "Right-handed. Off the backboard," he said. "Reverse layup." He dribbled up the drive but ran in a wide arc toward the basket, and without turning around tried to toss the ball to the sweet spot on the left. This was a tough shot for Phillip. While his momentum continued to carry him forward, he had to lift the ball back over his right shoulder. It was another piece of misdirection and a joyful combination of coordination and timing. As he looked back over his head, the ball ricocheted off the backboard and into the basket.

Greg picked the ball up. "You don't think that will work, do you?"

"You never know," Phillip smiled. "Show me what you've got."

"Yeah, yeah," Greg said, dribbling at the end of the driveway. He was pounding the ball, again and again, and looking down at the cement. Then he rose up and drove to and under the basket. The ball went up and wedged between the rim and backboard.

"Good try," Phillip said and slowly repeated each letter in its own space. "H O R S."

They both walked under the basket and looked up.

"Now you've done it," Phillip said.

"Any ideas?"

"I can't reach it."

"Me either."

The afternoon felt deflated. The silence was all around.

"Just a second," Phillip said, and he stepped to the garage door, reached down for the handle, and pulled up. The door rolled slowly back on its tracks. His father had gone to some meeting, leaving one side of the garage empty. Phillip took a rake from its clamp on the wall. "Let's try this," he said and poked the ball with the rake handle. At first the handle just skipped off the ball. Then Phillip aimed more purposefully, jabbed up into the ball's center, and it fell loose. Greg grabbed the ball, and Phillip returned the rake.

"Got time to finish?" Greg asked.

"Yeah," Phillip said. "My mom said till supper."

"I'm supposed to be back sooner," Greg said. "But I'm not stopping here. You're going to crack."

"Get out of here," Phillip said. "I'm on a roll. You're a goner." They each laughed, and Phillip pulled the rope at the side of the garage door, then stepped outside and held the handle as it lowered.

"My turn," Phillip said. Greg threw him the ball, and Phillip tried a shot from the left corner. It missed. Greg sunk a jump shot six feet from the sidewalk. Phillip missed.

"That's your S," Greg said. "Told you so." His face beamed. "I can see that crack getting wider and wider." Greg puffed his chest and continued to look at Phillip and grin. "Oooo," he raised a hand above his eyes. "The light through that crack is blinding me."

"It's not over," Phillip said and rolled Greg the ball.

"S, S," Greg said and tried to hit a shot from the sidewalk, another twelve feet beyond the foul line. It never reached the rim. There were a couple times over the summer when a few tenth graders played with them. They could make the sidewalk shot— at least the ball got to the rim and had a chance of going in. But for Greg and Phillip, it was almost always out of reach.

"Gave me an opening," Phillip said and dribbled the ball across the driveway from the left to the right. Just as he was reaching the center of the drive, he said, "Hook," and lifted the ball with his right hand, up and over his head, and it dropped right in. "Swish!"

"No, no," Greg said. "You know the rules. You have to call it before the ball leaves your hand."

"I know," Phillip said, "but isn't that the sweetest sound?"

"No," Greg said. "The sweetest sound is when you miss."

"You're playing with fire," Phillip said.

"I'm a fireman," Greg taunted. "Watch this." And he dribbled across the drive, brought the ball up in a fluid hook shot, and like a plane leaving the runway it effortlessly lifted, reached its apex, then surrendered to gravity and fell into the basket's center. "Swish," Greg shouted. "Take that!"

Phillip picked up the ball and dribbled around the court. He dribbled and dribbled.

"You lost?" Greg said.

"No. Just thinking. Just thinking how to send you home." He moved to the right side of the basket. "Okay," Phillip said. "Left-handed."

This time he couldn't dribble across the court. He could do several things with his left hand, but dribbling on the move wasn't one of them. So he stood on the right with his back to the basket and then took a big step across the center and brought the ball up in his left hand. Unlike a hook shot from the other side, this one felt wobbly. He hadn't as much feel in his left hand, and his fingers in his left couldn't spread and grip as well. But, if he didn't rush himself, he could execute a smooth left-handed hook that felt like a poor cousin of his right.

The ball dropped above the rim and bounced right and left. Then it rolled around the rim and fell through. Phillip grabbed the ball as it dropped from the net. He turned to Greg, "Put out that fire, big guy" and passed the ball.

Greg said nothing. He took the ball, dribbled it a bit, then went through the same routine as Phillip. But Greg's hook had more force, hit the backboard at an angle, and missed the basket completely.

"E," Greg said. "No cigar."

"Yep," Phillip said. "Just ONE champion."

"This time," Greg said.

"Yep, this time."

"Tomorrow?" Greg asked.

"Maybe. I still have the rest of those study questions, math and that essay."

"Get it done and call me," Greg said.

"Yep. Maybe."

Greg turned and headed across the street. Phillip noticed that the street lamp had turned on. The sky was getting darker.

He tried a shot from the sidewalk, but it didn't reach the rim. *Maybe next year*, he thought and took the ball inside.

Fran Baer

Rain

Marilyn Lorenz

Sometimes it is lovely when it rains.
You can stand at the window and be glad
to be dry, and safe, and watching.

You can get the ironing done that you've put off
for months, make a list of your passwords
and hide it somewhere, answer phone calls
and read.

Peanut butter and jelly is good for you
on a rainy day, and it's okay to sit down,
turn on something electronic, and find out
what streets are flooded, even if you had
no intention of going out.

Yes, sometimes it's lovely when it rains.
Even if all you do is curl up gratefully,
and nap.

Poet's Sonnet

Thelma Naylor

Fate forces to compose in simple verse
expressions for those thoughts we contemplate.
It seems like an affliction most perverse
but pray, how else should we communicate?

The work of sifting words for rhythmic play
perceived by many as a splendid gift,
is gold when we profound beliefs convey
concealed in forms so lovely and succinct.

Melodic cadence meant to hypnotize
and lull the senses into reverie,
ensures that what's delivered in such guise
will ageless, trancelike and ethereal be.

Such mesmerizing power may explain
the adoration certain poets claim.

Sandy Dimke

A Trip Outside

Fran Baer

Dianne Appell

Searching for Birdies and Eagles

James A Mallory

The stranger is perched on the splintered, dark gray bridge railing. Its glossy black wings spread out like Batman's cape. Its thin neck elongates, and the sharp tannish-orange beak points skyward.

I've never seen a bird like this before. I pause from my golf game to study it. Out of the corner of my eye I spot a similar bird, head bobbing up and down as it moves under the bridge that spans the lagoon. I burn the images in my mind. I will continue my research at home.

Google takes me to the website of the Hilton Head Island Audubon Society. A gallery of bird photos reveals that I had encountered an anhinga—a snakebird or water turkey or American darter—a common species on the island. Birds are bit players in my hometown of Detroit; they are center stage on the island. I learn that more than two hundred bird types call Hilton Head home.

I also discover a new way to enjoy golf.

★ ★ ★

Mark Twain said, "Golf is a good walk spoiled." I've used more profane descriptions of my game. Not any more. The curiosity piqued by my first sighting of the snakebird now provide me with a way to make sure that my hours on the fairways are never times of frustration. I even downloaded the Audubon app on my phone, just in case I need to do quick research.

I now recognize the red tail hawk's shriek and the squawking of the crows, warning that an adversary is nearby. The aerial theatrics of the warring birds are a thing of marvel, as are the other ways birds look out for each other.

Consider the four snakebirds that I see circling clockwise above a slow floating alligator. The birds switch to a counter-clockwise pattern and swoop ever closer to the water. Are they plotting revenge for the death of a fellow anhinga—the one that a golfer saw the day before caught in the crushing grip of an alligator?

I once failed to appreciate the frantic cawing of crows as they darted in the air or sat in nearby trees, and almost missed what I think is the grandest bird of all. A movement behind me caught my attention. I saw a large body skimming the surface of a nearby pond. The white-feathered head jutted forward. Widespread wings and the white tail let me know I am within yards of a bald eagle soaring up to its nest. It is like watching a 747 jetliner lift off the airport tarmac. The only disappointment is that my excitement of seeing the great bird keeps me from getting to my phone in time to snap a picture. Thankfully, the eagle and its mate make periodic appearances above the course where I live.

And what about the two turkeys standing sentry in a semi-clearing on an off-island golf course in Bluffton? It is late afternoon when I spot about a dozen large birds emerge from they woods. They slowly strut closer, finally stopping to forage, scratching and pecking the earth. Two of the huge birds, one on the left and the other on the right, lift their long necks high, scouting around to make sure that they do not wind up like their farm-raised distant cousins.

★ ★ ★

Birds are stalkers, too.

I watch a white heron standing monument-still in the marsh of my home course, oblivious to the golfers studying it from the tee box. It deftly lifts its thin legs one at a time. The neck extends. Before I can blink, the bird's beak thrusts into the murky water and snatches up a slimy morsel.

Yes, birds are crafty creatures. I no longer leave my peanut butter crackers in the open bins on my cart. I have watched, one time too many, a crow land on the cart and snatch my crackers while I am on the putting green. The last straw came when a thief entered my cart, grabbed an unopened package, got with some of his friends, opened it, and ate the snack that was to get me through the last nine holes.

★ ★ ★

One bird sighting did spoil my walk, or ride, if you will. As I step out of the cart on the 18th fairway of my home course, trying to decide whether I left my second—maybe it's my third—shot in a spot where I could hit onto the green, I am distracted by a low-flying great blue heron. The elegant bird, its regal head with white, black and gray plumage tucked back, soars gracefully by—neck arrow straight toward its destination, legs aimed toward its departure point. My eyes notice the stick-thin legs. Dangling from the right one is a thread-like piece of cargo that I am sure the heron had no intention of picking up. I feel helpless. I am frustrated. I still wonder what, if anything, the great blue was able to do to remove the fishhook and line from its leg.

The great blue's struggle left me more conscientious about picking up the trash that careless golfers tossed around the course. We humans habitually disregard how our habits affect the nature that we so love.

On the course, necessary birdies remain elusive for me. Coveted eagles do not enter the equation. I'm not bothered, though. I know that at any time, I can look up, and around, to savor the beauty of the real thing.

Whispering Breeze

Thelma Naylor

Soft as a goodnight kiss,
each whisper,
a choreography.

Dozing pansies, scatter out of bed,
into the erratic flight of butterflies.
A lone camellia, startled,
glides away as a cardinal.

Time-bronzed leaves quiver,
dangling, shimmering, not ready to fall.
Lacy tufts of Spanish moss,
sway in time on graceful limbs.

Jet-black cape outstretched,
a vulture hovers,
suspended by a whisper all its own.

I dance along,
borne by the breeze.

Cross My Heart

Bev Moss Haedrich

I was feeling a bit indulgent after working all week from a rustic rented cabin on Lake Marion. Touching my wrist, I realized I'd left my watch behind. Well, judging today's distance against yesterday's time is going to be difficult. Never mind, I thought. Time is on my side.

Warming up is key to enjoying a morning walk. Not just loosening up the muscles and joints in my arms, legs and lower back, but clearing those stringy fibrous cobwebs that fill and clutter the mind. Those self-doubts and people dramas that invade our business lives so easily. I systematically try to dislodge each of them so my walk is light spirited and satisfying. Sometimes I walk to spend uninterrupted mind time with someone I miss, or calculate my options for the future, or plan my next vacation. But this was my last day at the cabin, and a leisurely stroll was my reward for a tough work week.

I had driven the back roads for days, wishing more than once that I'd latched my bike to its rack. I needed to get closer to the lake's edge. It is massive in size and spans five counties. Imagining the record-size large mouth bass hooked from its depths, I wanted to see more. Stopping once, I scurried across the road, risking jail time or maybe the slap of a trespassing fine, to snip a cracked boll of cotton from a large field ripe with the plump soft puffs for a friend in New England. I wanted him to experience the texture of this Carolina landscape I loved and now called home. That plucked raw cotton was so much better than a flat postcard.

As my momentum builds toward a comfortable stride, I could feel that exhilarating sensation as the week's pressures release into the surrounding atmosphere. I exhale. The meetings and deadlines, the multitude of people I had met are rapidly leaving me now. Or am I leaving them as my pulse and pace quicken? Walking provides freedom for me, always has.

My arch-support tennis shoes scuff the dry gravel road and I look down. A grayish cloud billows around my feet, and I notice my loose lace. I kneel to double knot it and remember the childhood times spent with my cousin. One of our shoelaces was always dangling, causing us frequent halts in our animated conversations. I remember it as if it were yesterday.

"Mama knows everything," I said smiling.

"She told us to double tie these things," my cousin Deana said, squatting to tighten both of hers.

"But we didn't do it," we sang in unison.

Funny how the things we learn as a child can stay with us throughout life. I look down at my colorful laces, double tied, and smile.

As children Deana and I would go on picnics, leaving all our boy cousins behind. Mama would pack us a lunch to take on our adventure. Sometimes she fixed apple butter sandwiches on Wonder Bread, but usually it was peanut butter and her homemade grape or strawberry jelly. No matter which sandwich she made, it always tasted better outdoors. She included a couple of apples from the trees in the yard, her chewy oatmeal cookies and Kool-Aid in a jar.

"You girls be careful now," she'd say, wagging her finger at us. She always ended by saying, "And don't be gone too long!"

When we heard those words, it was like the gates at the Kentucky Derby had flung open. We were off and running! We had plans, great plans of faraway places as our Keds hit the dirt road leading high up the hill and past the family cemetery. Once we were out of sight, we'd lie in the grass, looking up at the clouds. We were big girls and didn't want Mama seeing us take a break for fear she may not let us go again. We loved these excursions on our own.

"Look, look! It's a giraffe—see her long neck?" Deana whispered.

She kept pointing at it until I saw its head, long neck, body and tail, too. Why, we could nearly make out the brown and beige spots. Its pointy ears cocked outwardly, and we called its horns a crown. We laughed when a breeze sent the "tallest creature in the world" galloping off and fading into the clouds. We'd squeal with delight at a "dog" or a "cat" or "lion." We took turns pointing out animals and described each with such detail and enthusiasm, like the time a dinosaur's tail grew right before our eyes.

"SEE IT?" I shouted. "There, right there! See the big body, and over there is his tail!"

"I think I see it."

"You think? It's right there!" I said, wide-eyed and pointing with all my might. "Oh, look! Its tail is really getting big now!"

"Okay, I see it," Deana reluctantly said, holding her stomach. "I'm getting really hungry."

"Me, too."

We headed toward our favorite spot, and our chatter continued. We shared tales about our meanest teachers, and the things we'd do if we had half a chance. Nothing really bad but just enough, we hoped, to cause what we imagined as pure misery on our worst foes. An egg on the chair of ole Miss Cassell and not hard boiled either! We laughed at the thought of her walking the halls for the rest of the day with raw egg splattered across her backside. And that red haired boy who wouldn't leave us alone— tied shoelaces and watching him stumble would serve him just right! We giggled at our fantasies and promised to treasure our secrets crossing our hearts each time.

After walking what seemed miles for our skinny little legs, Deana said she could smell Mama's peanut butter and jelly sandwiches. I thought I could, too. Once we neared the barbed wire fence that separated us from an unpredictable bull and our favorite place to picnic, we checked our clothing for any signs of red. I had no intention of playing matador to this huge beast! And besides, hadn't our mothers or somebody been chased once by this very bull? We were always careful going in. We squatted and had to crawl between prickly wires, holding onto a rickety fence post, before dashing into the nearby woods.

"Ah, we're safe!"

"Yes!" Deana shot her arm toward the sky in victory. "We did it!"

We searched for a broom to sweep the forest floor clean. It had to be just the right length for our little arms yet sturdy enough to clear layers of pine needles and dried oak leaves from our make-shift kitchen where we'd eat our picnic lunch. We'd sit on a fallen log and declare the space as the perfect place to sit and talk. We'd reminisce about everything in our young lives, from boy cousins to weeding Aunt Mildred's flowerbed. We promised—swearing wasn't aloud—we would never have phlox in our gardens when we grew up and got married.

"I'm so hungry! Let's eat before that bull sees us."

On more than a few occasions our exits had been made in haste when one of us swore we felt the earth tremble under the weight of pounding hooves. With a *cross my hear* we were convinced they were headed in our direction. Once, we left so quickly, grabbing our half-eaten lunch, that I scraped the inside of my knee on the rusty barbed wire. A half-century later that scar still lingers as proof of having fought off the raging bull.

At around eight or nine years old, hiking up and down rolling hills and skipping on and off of dirt paths near Mama and Papa's, proved better than any game our cousins could dream up. Except for maybe catching lightning bugs in the early evening. Some-times I'd head over the furthest hill to Thomas' General Store with one of my cousins where orange sherbet Push-Ups were kept ice cold in a chest freezer along the wall. Once I'd made my choice, the quarter that had been safely stashed deep in the pocket of my shorts was handed over to Mrs. Thomas.

"Be sure and tell your Mama hi for me now," she'd say, taking the wrapper off the frozen treat for me. "I'll see her at church on Sunday now."

I loved taking walks even back then. It was a break from adults, sweeping, and other divvied-up chores. It was a time when Deana and I could escape the boys, too, and talk about girl stuff like the pretty material in Mama's latest quilt or how much we loathed weeding the phlox that lined both sides of her sidewalk.

I chuckle, feeling grateful for the fond memories of my childhood and the sweet accomplice who shared picnics in the forest and dodged creatures, both small and humongous, with me. Yes, walks can sometimes be surreal, transporting us to dream-like places. Now is this my third or fourth lap around this dusty trail? It didn't matter. I felt like walking a bit longer, thankful for leaving my watch behind. Cross my heart

Carol Linneman

Nest #26

~

Carol Linneman

"My nest, my nest, I have a nest!" So much excitement in the voice of a seven year old upon learning of his sea turtle nest adoption! "Mama, when can I go to the beach? I want to visit my nest."

"Soon, Carpenter," his mother answered with a smile as she closed the email with the nest information. "Your Spring Break with Mama Lee and Papa Mac is next week. You know Mama Lee will take you every day. You will be able to visit all you want."

"Awesome! I can't wait! I just can't wait," he exclaimed while jumping up and down.

Spring Break finally arrived, and so did Carpenter from Atlanta. Almost immediately he was off to see his nest, encircled with yellow plastic ribbon attached to three white round poles. A triangular orange sign identified the spot as "Loggerhead Turtle Nesting Area. Eggs, Hatchlings, Adults, and Carcasses are Protected by Federal & State Laws." One of the poles bore the number 26—Carpenter had found his nest.

"It's here, right here, Mama Lee! Look!" He ran his hand gently along the yellow tape, moving from pole to pole. "If I stand next to my number, will you take a picture? I'll keep it forever!"

Mama Lee clicked away while Carpenter yelled, "Boo-yah! I love that they protect the nests, Mama Lee. I'll help them watch my nest for sure."

The protection efforts were led by Hilton Head Island Coastal Discovery Museum's Sea Turtle Protection Project as part of the South Carolina Department of Natural Resources, managed by local marine biologist Amber Kuehn. Amber and her team of patrollers ventured out EARLY every morning during nesting season to identify, protect, and inventory over three hundred nests along the shoreline. Carpenter sometimes got up early to meet the team at his nest.

As part of the program, an adoption curriculum was spear-headed by Andrea Siebold in an effort to not only raise funds for the endeavor but also to promote awareness of the plight of the endangered Loggerheads. It included a plan to educate island residents and visitors, and Carpenter was determined to assist.

Andrea regularly updated adopters with information about the life of sea turtles, and as nests were laid, assigned each adopter a specific nest by number to enhance an ownership experience. She also emailed frequent progress details and pictures to each adopter.

Carpenter took the effort seriously. Since he knew that many out-of-state visitors were not aware of the sea turtle habitats, he saw to it that any beach-goers approaching *his* nest would hear about sea turtles and learn to respect them. He memorized his fact list. "Mama sea turtles, some weigh three hundred pounds, come to the beach every spring. They dig deep holes with their back flippers and lay around one hundred eggs about the size of golf balls. Then they cover up the hole with sand and go back to the ocean. Don't touch the nest—only look at it or take a picture—and never touch or poke a mama turtle if you see one. I hope I'm here when the eggs hatch."

Carpenter's heart for the turtles surfaced through his dimpled smile and expressive hand gestures. He would press on whenever he sensed an interested audience. "And, when it's dark, don't use flashlights or flash cameras on the beach. You'll scare a mama coming to lay eggs, and she'll go back to the water. Or, if babies are hatching and leaving their nest, they'll follow your light instead of the ocean's and get lost. It's OK if you use one of the new red-light type flashlights."

If an audience remained hooked, he would pull his wide-brimmed Salty Dog hat further down over his face to shield big brown eyes and fair skin and become even more engaging, his lanky frame bouncing as he *preached.*

"Some people leave outside house lights on—wronggg! The babies might go to those houses and fall into pools. Then the babies use up energy and get too tired to make a sea journey and will die. Another thing, if you dig in the sand, always fill in the hole when you leave so a turtle doesn't get stuck in it. And knock down the sand castles so that you don't block the way of one of the babies. When I'm here, I fill holes and smash down sand walls!"

One afternoon Mama Lee was walking along the water's edge with Carpenter. Suddenly, Carpenter took off like lightning down the beach after what, his grandmother did not know. It turned out that he had seen a plastic bag being carried along with the wind.

Returning with the bag in hand, he expounded, "This bag could kill a turtle that might eat it thinking it was a jellyfish. Why do people leave trash on the beach anyway?"

Later in the summer Carpenter was fortunate to return two days after his nest hatched. On the third post-hatch day, he was invited by the Sea Turtle Patrol to observe the inventory of his nest. After digging up the nest with gloved hands, one of the patrol members rescued five little hatchlings left behind.

Carpenter exclaimed, "Are you kidding me? They're alive; they're alive; see them, Mama Lee and Papa Mac?"

The hatchlings were placed on the open sand so they could make their way to the water. Carpenter learned the importance of the hatchlings crawling to the water on their own. It was necessary in order for their built-in GPSs to begin working, leading them towards a life's journey to and through the seas!

During story-time in his second grade class, Carpenter proudly shares pictures and relates his summer turtle experience. He concludes with, "Do you know that my girl baby turtles will come back to Hilton Head when they're grown up to build nests and lay eggs on the same beach where they hatched? And guess how old they'll be when they come back?" He pauses. "About twenty-five years old!" Carpenter imparts his knowledge, not as a kid with earned bragging rights, but as one who earnestly cares about the turtles and their future.

Living On a Water Planet

Jim Riggs

I watch as a storm pummels our island.
   Dancing fronds oscillate, gyrating.
      Tropical palms and live oaks confirm their strength
         bending, whipping, almost unbreakable.

A storm anoints my world,
   streaming rain
      limiting my vision
         to a million vertical lines.

Becoming ten again,
   loating a carefully carved boat
      in a water-filled gutter
         rushing beside the hilly street, drifting toward ocean.

After a heavy rain,
   I gather a can of night crawlers,
      removing them from the pavement oven,
         recycling them as fish bait.

During a summer rain, I lie sheltered
   in my tent, dry, surrounded by cloudbursts,
      listening to raindrops pounding on nylon,
         feeling safe and comfortable.

I paddle in a summer rain, protected by rain gear,
   water dripping off my cap,
      watching raindrops explode on the river
      mimicking miniature volcanoes.

I watch sun shining on an eastern sky
   softly touching gently falling raindrops,
      prisms bending light, spectrums,
      forming a magical rainbow.

Walking in a prairie
   after a summer rain,
      I celebrate fresh, warm-weather flowers,
      outlined in dew-like drops.

I live on a water planet,
   where rain, streams, rivers, lakes,
      marshes, estuaries, and oceans
      enrich my life.

Susan Proto

Hunting Trees

R. Elliott Anderson

Why have I become obsessed with loblolly pines and live oak trees?

Clearly, it's Matthew and the whipping that hurricane administered to Hilton Head Island's trees—shoving them onto houses, straddling them across streets, barricading driveways, bending them into lagoons and practically clearcutting peaceful maritime forests.

Before the Big Blow, I did not know these ubiquitous pines were called *loblolly*, a moniker derived from an old English word for mud hole. It seems the trees like moist ground, even swampy conditions, so it's kind of easy to see how they got their peculiar name. But if you don't like loblolly you can call them *Pinus Taeda*. These skyscrapers are predominant in South Carolina and are valuable when converted into fence posts, utility poles, pulpwood and lumber. They are trees grown on large tree plantations to be cut down for money. Soaring upward, anchored by a sturdy taproot, individually they don't catch your eye as things of beauty like a live oak or maybe a spreading chestnut tree. At eye level they are mostly bark and some are so skinny they look like giant toothpicks stuck in Mother Nature's teeth.

We know loblollies best by their needles, which fall in little packets of three, on your roof and driveway, in the rain gutters, the grass, the shrubs, and your hair if you stand under them awhile. If that's not bad enough, they clutter up the streets, driveways, golf courses and grass with large pine cones that have sharp little pine knives sticking out of them. Best not pick them up with your bare hands. Guess we shouldn't forget the pollen, which in the spring spreads a patina of yellowish-green dust on everything inside and outside the house.

Now in their favor, pine forests are a sign of the South, home to about thirteen different species; when standing together the trees are stately and handsome. And they could well get a Good Housekeeping award for their environmental cleanup duties, since they are major contributors to CO_2 sequestration. Destroying the loblollies would have a significant negative

impact on our environmental health. Hopefully they won't all get blown down or cut down; as long as they stay erect, they are friendly trees with our interest at heart.

However, when I went hunting for distinguished loblollies in or near the Lowcountry, I discovered only one tree, and that was inland in Augusta, Georgia, on the 17th hole of Augusta National Golf Course, named the Eisenhower Tree because President Eisenhower, a member of Augusta National, rather consistently hit the tree while playing that particular hole. Out of frustration Ike asked the club's Board to cut the tree down. The Board demurred, but eventually Ike's plea came to pass when lightening struck the tree and it had to be removed. So like Ike himself, the Eisenhower Tree is but a memory.

When it comes to hurricanes, we think of *named storms*; and when it comes to live oak trees we think of *named trees*. Thankfully, most of these named trees have outfoxed the named storms. Live oaks are survivors and can look forward to hundreds of years on Earth despite what the weather dishes out. Unlike the loblollies they crouch closer to the ground, spreading out horizontally rather than shooting upward to defy the wind. Countless loblollies lose the battle; they are toppled like dominoes, mud hole roots and all.

Considering the disparity of remarkable loblollies, I went hunting for named live oaks in the Lowcountry, from the Golden Isles of Georgia to the outskirts of Charleston, but I realized I had to cherry-pick my targets because of the number of marvelous trees within my geographical parameter.

Along the way, I picked up a little background on the trees such as their Latin name: *Quercus Virginiana*. What a great name for a tree, and you can even pronounce it. It's common knowledge they are called *live* because they stay green all year long even though they are not evergreens. They do drop scads of leaves in the early spring, as anyone with a leaf blower will tell you, but the new leaves pull a quick-change act and emerge rapidly. They like the Lowcountry climate and are rather tolerant of salty conditions; you can see many huddled along the shore that have adapted to the wind and waves. Although stunted looking, the limbs are as zigzagged as ever and when jumbled together can even appear a bit spooky.

Another thing I learned is they are not really as old as everyone says. Talking them up to be a thousand years old is overkill. Maybe three hundred to five hundred for some of them; not that that's trivial. They are very sturdy trees for sure. But they are not valuable for their wood, like loblollies, because the wood is too dense to cut or work with easily. You could take a live oak board and throw it into a lagoon and it would sink like a brick. The wood, however, was used extensively in the wooden ship era capitalizing on its strength for interior parts. The USS Constitution (Old Ironsides), the oldest navy vessel still afloat, contains a good deal of live oak in its structure, some of it remaining from the original construction in 1797. But the outside walls are made of multiple layers of white oak so thick you could bounce a cannonball off them. That's not all; the U. S. Navy's first warships contained live oak harvested from St. Simons Island, and the last surviving whale ship, the Charles Morgan, anchored at Mystic Seaport in Connecticut, was refurbished not long ago using live oak in its interior structure. Unfortunately, the trees don't stand up to every hurricane. The live oak used in the reconstruction was cast off from ravaged trees resulting from Hurricane Katrina.

But the named oaks I viewed are all very old and have survived a great many storms. The Plantation Oak in Jekyll Island, Georgia's historic district, is estimated to be 375 years old. Typical of live oaks, it is more expansive than tall, and the heavy branches sag to the ground, developing props that stabilize the massive spread. The Plantation Oak has been singled out for recognition, but there are hundreds of beautiful live oaks in the historic area. At night spotlights illuminate their twisted architecture, turning the grounds into a magical mystery tour.

Just a little north in Brunswick, Georgia, is the famous Lover's Oak located at the intersection of Albany and Prince streets in the historic section of Brunswick. The hype claims the tree is nine hundred years old (That's the 12th century, folks.), which I personally doubt, but arborists say it was there at the time of the signing of the Constitution, which is believable. Its longevity is amazing because it is in the middle of the street. Unfortunately, it lost a limb when not long ago it was hit by a semi truck.

Other named trees have survived in the middle of the road. The Fraser Oak in Sea Pines has a very handsome setting in Fraser Circle located in the heart of an intersection of four roads. We can't overlook the Carolina Shores Oak smack in the middle of the entrance road to Carolina Shores subdivision in Beaufort. The tree had a star turn in the movie *The War,* which featured a disputed tree house perched among its crooked branches. It may have been the oak prominent in *Forrest Gump*, but controversy surrounds where the Gump tree is located.

Speaking of prominent oaks, the live oak on the former Cherry Hill Plantation in Beaufort was named South Carolina's Heritage Tree in 2013. When I hunted for it down a dusty dead end road, I had a devil of a time finding it; there were so many large oaks in the area, you might say I was up a tree.

Development plans have been revised to show respect for live oaks. The Harbour Town yacht basin, originally designed to be round, was redrawn to accommodate what is now known as the Liberty Oak, perhaps the most famous live oak on Hilton Head Island. The lagoon design in Jarvis Creek Park on the island preserves a significant oak that is in a prominent place on the edge of the water. And the gracious live oaks surrounding the Frampton Plantation House in Yemassee, South Carolina, were saved from being cleared away to make room for a truck stop.

Two oaks that have dominated the list of large oaks to see are the Middleton Oak in Middleton Place on Charleston's outskirts and the Angel Oak on John's Island along the road to Kiawah. My impression of the Middleton Oak is that it is a wounded warrior struggling to maintain past glory. The tree has lost two huge limbs that constituted a significant part of its heft, and though it has an envied location along the flooded rice field at Middleton Place, there are several eye-catching oaks on the property that have managed to stay in better shape. If you don't check the property map, You can mistake any number of trees for the honored Middleton Oak.

The Angel Oak gets my vote as the largest, most complex and awe inspiring tree in the Lowcountry and probably the South Atlantic coast. It has huge, lengthy, crooked, octopus-like arms that run along the ground and into the air above. It probably takes up half a football field. No mistake, it's a charmed tree that has side-stepped the two major predators on Earth, Mother Nature and, well, us. When a proposed condo development threatened the Angel Oak, citizen groups and the City of Charleston purchased the acreage around the revered tree and stiff-armed the developers. The oak has become a touristic success and cars line the parking area and nearby road; visitors amble around and under the convoluted structure. To crown its achievement, it has been awarded its own gift shop and picnic tables on the grounds, complete with porta-potties.

When it comes to sheer perfection of proportion and stateliness the Talbird Oak in Hilton Head Plantation would have brought tears to Joyce Kilmer's eyes had he been able to see it. Alas, there are no live oaks in New Jersey.

The tree has a well-known backstory. The Talbird plantation house was ordered to be burned down during the Revolutionary War by British troops. The officer in charge allowed Mrs. Talbird, whose husband was a prisoner of the British, to move the furniture out and put it under a nearby oak tree before burning the house to the ground. The strange thing was the British officer in charge was Mrs. Talbird's brother-in-law, and she was nine months pregnant—giving birth the next day. Now as bad as losing the house seems, it was better they destroyed the house, which could be rebuilt, and left the tree unharmed, which couldn't be rebuilt—unless you wanted to wait three hundred years.

It would be easy to conclude that live oaks are only things of beauty when considered individually. Of course these magnificent trees have no comprehension of how imposing they are; august, spreading their crazed limbs covered with dangling Spanish Moss, in a way that's only for us. They have no conscious awareness. Only we have that. But as many photographers know, a procession of live oaks along plantation roads, the canopies over Savannah's squares, and arching limbs in places like Wormsloe Estate form ethereal settings that get iPhones clicking. Certainly, we can't ignore the enchanting aura of the angled trees when draped with epiphyte Spanish moss, especially in the evening hours when the scene can grow enchanting.

Hurricane Matthew's savage treatment of the trees that surround us generated my initial interest, particularly when the agonized remains cluttered our roadsides and open spaces.

In searching for trees, I originally was intrigued with only age and size. The loblollies drew attention first based on height and to some degree age, not by their individual overwhelming beauty. Soon enough live oaks in my eyes got measured by the aesthetics of the tree and its setting, regardless of age or the spread of their limbs or the amount of Spanish moss. All got credit for survivability from the outrageous winds of the inevitable storms, after all they are where they are. They cannot seek shelter when Mother Nature turns on herself in mindless destruction. The loblollies have a tough role to play; the live oaks dodge the terror, but as we know, not completely.

There are many live oaks worth visiting. Sea Pines Resort has fifteen of them mapped out; although I hunted down all of them, some could be recognized only because they are marked by commemorative wooden benches. The beautiful trees are plentiful in the Lowcountry and along the coast as far as Texas. You may have your own favorite live oak, but I doubt that you have your favorite loblolly pine.

Night Fishing

Jim Riggs

During the last years of his life my father-in-law, Harold Lott, regaled me with his youthful adventures paddling the Elk during an Easter trip to Minnesota. His stories and my trip merged into this piece of fiction about what might have happened in 1924. I read this story to Harold on his death bed and received a broad smile for my effort.

★ ★ ★

A moment before the light found us I heard Harold's loud whisper.

"Dump the sack."

I tied a quick square knot in the rope to close the gunnysack. Then I slid the bag full of rocks and illegal fish over the stern of the wooden jon boat. Henry beamed his bright flashlight toward shore. Our bag sank to the bottom of the Elk River. Henry's light shined in the eyes and off the badge of a game warden standing on the bank.

Henry rowed toward the rugged-looking man with the heavy salt and pepper mustache and the two day growth of beard. His hands rested on his hips. I could see the big black revolver in an open holster at his waist. I was scared.

"How you doing?" asked Henry.

The brawny officer responded, "What are you boys up to tonight?"

Henry was cool, like he was playing poker, holding a full house. He replied to the brawny man with the gun, "We're just out spearing some suckers and carp. Nothing illegal."

The warden flashed a spotlight into our boat, searching with the light and his eyes. He saw three dirty, wet, slimy, farm kids, two four prong barbed fish spears on long wooden poles, and lying in the bottom of the boat, three ten pound carp and two suckers half that big, nothing but rough fish. We knew the game warden wouldn't bother us about the carp and suckers, but we'd a been dead meat if he'd seen our sack of walleyes and northern pike.

We were all dressed in overalls, raggedy wool winter coats, and warm wool caps with earflaps. All of us had been in and out of the icy cold water of the Elk River many times during this chilly April night. I was just a kid. I'd be fifteen in a week. Henry was near to twenty and Harold was eighteen. I just hoped I wouldn't spend my birthday in the Sherburne County Jail.

It was 1924, and Minnesota's Elk River ran perfectly clear. The pretty river originated in the sand hills in central Minnesota, northwest of The Twin Cities. In those days, we could drink the water any day of the year. It was so slow-moving that sometimes it cut back on itself so after rowing for a mile we could throw a rock over the narrow neck of land and hit the water we'd been in an hour before.

With our flashlight it was easy to spot northern pike, catfish, carp, and suckers cruising the shallow water. By rowing and poling within range, we could sink our spears into their broad backs. If we were a might slow, we'd sometimes stick a spear in the tail. Then we had to push the spear down into the sandy bottom of the river and hold the powerful, wiggling fish there until it was exhausted. A fighting twenty-pound northern pike could easily break the handle, giving us a big search for a strong fish dragging half a spear. If we found it, the result was often a cold, wet race to grab the broken spear as a fierce predator with a mouth full of sharp teeth tried to rid itself of the cumbersome, barbed steel in its tail.

When the cold overpowered us we'd stop on a grassy bank, building a roaring fire, toasting our fronts and backs in the hot flames until our clothes started to steam and a feeling of warmth began oozing into our bones. In a half hour, we'd be a little less wet. We'd begin to feel blood flowing through our fingers again. Then, we'd climb back into the wooden boat and search for another torpedo-shaped northern pike to add to our gunny sack.

Henry and the game warden were chatting in the dark. Harold whispered in my ear. "Our illegal fish are tied up in a gunny sack at the bottom of Elk River. Why the hell doesn't Henry stop talking so the man can go home, and we can retrieve our fish and get back to spearing."

I whispered back, "My butt's freezing. It's time to build another fire and warm up."

The warden shined his light toward Harold and me. "What are you two whispering about?"

I tended to be tongue-tied, but at that moment I thought real quick. The truth pays, my momma always said. "I was just saying my butt is darn cold. We was hoping this conversation doesn't take all night."

"Are you getting wise with me?"

"No sir. I'm just feeling mighty cold, sir. You take your time."

"Well, I reckon I'll be on my way," he said. He eyed our catch, one more time. "Nice mess of fish, fellows. You gonna smoke them?"

"Sure, I reckon we'll smoke 'em," Henry responded. "They're pretty bony fried, but the bones don't seem to be no problem when we smoke 'em."

He sounded so calm. I was still scared that the warden had seen us dump that bag of game fish. I hoped he hadn't seen us spearing that last northern an hour ago? I didn't know how he coulda.

In the dark, I looked up at the officer. I could tell he wore a plaid Mackinaw and trapper hat with loose flaps. He was probably plenty warm. I glanced again at the big pistol. The man frightened me. I wondered if he would ever leave. I just wanted to get back in the Model T and go home. I wanted to crawl into dry, clean long Johns and know we were safe from the law. I had a vision of all three of us sharing a jail cell.

Harold and Henry still seemed composed. They kept yakking with the darned game warden as if he was a buddy from the next farm.

"Well, good luck fellows. It's good to see you're keeping your spears out of the northern pike. Get rid of these suckers and carp and the game fish will do better. I'm proud we've got honest, law-abiding young men like you around. Good luck to you."

The warden turned and walked away and we pushed the boat back into the current.

"Let's just spear suckers for an hour or so," Harold suggested softly. "Give that damned game warden a chance to get long gone before we get our sack and go home."

"I'm scared, Harold. What if he arrests us? We ain't got no money for a fine. He'll throw us all in jail."

"Don't worry," said Harold, Mr. Cool as a Cucumber. "They ain't gonna put a bunch of kids in jail. They'll just slap our hands and tell us not to do it again. Anyway, he ain't gonna catch us. We're going sucker spearing for a couple of hours and give him a chance to get a long ways from here."

Two hours later our sacks of fish were on the floor of the back seat of the Model T. We were almost home and I was starting to relax. Then I saw the car parked just a quarter of a mile from our house.

"Harold, there's a car beside the road. It's that game warden, waiting for us. We didn't fool him. He's going to arrest us."

"Shut up. Open the back door and throw those fish in the ditch. We're still okay if all he finds is suckers and carp."

As our Ford passed the parked car, we recognized Bert's old Buick. Its windows were all fogged up from some heavy breathing inside.

Pulling up along side, Henry rolled down his window and hollered. "Hey, Bert. What 'cha doing out here in the middle of the night." It took a few moments for Bert to get himself straightened around and open the window to respond.

"Go away. Can't you guys let a fellow have any peace and quiet?"

That's when we noticed that there was someone else in the car. Elsie peaked over his shoulder.

"A ... Sorry, Bert. We was out fishn' 'n thought you was the game warden. Frank, run back and get them fish. We got to be going, Bert. We got fish to clean. I'm sure glad it was you instead of the game warden. We might of had us some serious trouble."

Biking on Hilton Head Island

~

Norma VanAmberg

Touring Hilton Head Island on a bicycle is an excellent way to view the natural beauty of this barrier island. Even the main road, William Hilton Parkway, offers landscaped medians and entrances to subdivisions full of colorful, flowering plants. Plus you get great exercise doing it. A brunch or dinner break at one of the many eateries provides a refreshing stop along your way.

After a long ride to the Coligny Beach area on a hot day, a friend and I treated ourselves to a hearty omelet and pancake breakfast at the popular Skillets restaurant. We knew we could pedal and perspire away a good amount of the calories, pumping our way down the beach to get into Sea Pines. Then we could walk our bikes on one of the beach access points to reach the pathway and enjoy some tree shade on the return trip.

Bicycling on a subtropical island is an adventure. You can discover a great blue heron lifting off from the edge of a lagoon, stop to join some people watching an alligator sun itself on an embankment, or inhale the scent of the ocean air wafting on a welcome breeze.

Once I got my bike with gears, which makes pedaling longer distances on inclines more comfortable, I was ready to climb the Charles E. Fraser Bridge over Broad Creek. It offers a panoramic view of the Palmetto Bay area when you enter or leave the Cross Island Parkway.

I like to head off Palmetto Bay Road toward the marina and stop for a cool beverage at outdoor seating by the Black Marlin or Charleston Crab Company restaurants there.

When I go bicycling mid-island in Shelter Cove, I stop at the Veterans Memorial at Shelter Cove Community Park. I don't have a family member who served, but I do remember the friends of my generation who fought and even died in Vietnam. In addition to pausing at the memorial, visitors can relax on benches overlooking Broad Creek or meander the trail on the grounds.

Members of the Lowcountry Adventures Meet Up, a group I belong to, got a history lesson about Hilton Head as a bonus during a bike ride down Beach City Road. After stopping briefly at the site of Fort Howell, built by U.S. troops during the Civil War to protect Hilton Head, we headed to nearby Fish Haul Park. This is the site of a work-in-progress, Mitchelville Freedom Park, which was launched in 2011. A group of volunteer citizens organized the Mitchelville Preservation Project to create the commemorative park on the site of the original first town established by freed slaves during the Civil War.

The Town of Hilton Head Island acquired the 16.55-acre property overlooking Port Royal Sound in 1998 and opened a passive park there in 2005. Project volunteers have developed displays full of information, scheduled events, and replicas of Mitchelville's original tiny houses, tool sheds, and garden plots.

The Toni Morrison Society's Bench by the Road project, honoring the Nobel Laureate poet, placed a bench at Mitchelville. The black metal seat, installed in 2013, commemorates the founding of Mitchelville. The plaque states: "Let this seat be your resting place to gain composure from life's journey and to commune with the surrounding lingering spirits of the past way makers."

We all agreed this was a moving experience and a place to plan a picnic outing. A pier for viewing the scenery or fishing, a small picnic pavilion, a wooded trail leading to a beach, and rest rooms are available.

Pathways and beach

The town and community leaders' dedication to creating about sixty miles of public pathways and nature trails—along with the nearly fifty miles of paths behind gated communities—has earned Hilton Head national recognition. The League of American Bicyclists named it a gold-level Bicycle Friendly Community, one of twenty-five such cycling communities in the nation.

When visiting family or friends want to bike on the beach, I recommend using bikes with fatter tires because these are best for the hard-packed sand along the ocean. Nearly thirty rental shops on the island offer a variety of approximately 15,000 bicycles. Some offer guided tours, and there are local biking clubs that coordinate weekly rides for bikers of all skill levels.

As we age, balance issues and physical ailments can sometimes make it difficult to enjoy cycling. But there are three-wheel bikes for adults, as well as those built for two, and even ones with reclining seats to ease undue strain on the back or knees. Babies and pets can tag along in attached carriers.

With a history of environmental leadership, the Hilton Head community continues to promote and support the green movement and family-friendly activities. Construction of multi-use pathways began on the island when development continued to grow in the early 1970s.

Access to the beach is available from the public parks, the resort hotels and other lodgings in the gated communities. Signs point the way for the general public at entries along the pathway network, and maps are available at the town hall, the Chamber of Commerce, at other information outlets, and online.

Benefits of cycling

Remember the popular adage, "You never forget how to ride a bike"? Perhaps it's time to try it again if it's been a while since you pedaled. If you need to be motivated, a *Harvard Health Letter* article published in 2016 cited five main physical benefits of cycling. I agree that I feel as though I have had a good cardio-vascular workout and sweated out some toxins by the time I return from a ride.

Plus, "It's socially oriented, it's fun, and it gets you outside and exercising," says Dr. Clare Safran-Norton, a physical therapist at Harvard-affiliated Brigham and Women's Hospital.

Before doing any strenuous exercise, it is wise to check with your doctor if you are being treated for a heart condition, arthritis, osteoporosis, or have had a recent bone fracture. I found the seat height should allow a slight bend at your knee for efficient execution and comfort in pedaling.

Instead of driving to the post office or the grocery store, I sometimes ride my bike to save on gas and make the time to exercise. Safety is always an important consideration. I narrowly missed having a mishap on a narrow street in town when someone opened a car door just as I was about to pass by.

In addition to obeying all rules of the road as the driver of a vehicle (bike), I cross busy streets and highways at intersections with traffic lights when possible. Sometimes I walk the bike to feel more secure doing that, which makes me a pedestrian. Vehicles have the right of way unless signs indicate they must yield to pedestrians. Safety and personal responsibility are especially important at all times. In fact, *The Island Packet,* the local newspaper, ran a series of articles in March 2017 about the number of bike and pedestrian fatalities in Beaufort County. There were four cyclist fatalities on Hilton Head between August 2016 and March 2017. Twenty of the twenty-eight fatal bicycle and pedestrian wrecks on Hilton Head from 2000 to 2016 occurred on a dark road at night.

So obey all rules of the road, wear a helmet for protection in case of any mishaps, and take precautions with reflective clothing and lights and a headlight if you ride at night. Don't drink and ride either! Happy trails!

When the Sand Whispers

Judy Groves

It was a beautiful Saturday morning on Hilton Head Island, and Rosemary, a member of the "Ride On!" bike club, was happy as a lark to be out biking with her friends again. Today they were on one of her favorite bike trails, and, at eighty-three, she was still going strong! Rosemary laughed. Her younger friend, Gracie, biking behind her, was already huffing and puffing.

"How do you do it, Rosemary? I'm already tired," Gracie said.

"I get my energy and inspiration at the beach when the sand whispers to me."

"The sand whispers to you...how?"

"Well, when a grain of sand is kissed by the wind, it whispers a personal message to the one who should hear it. One thing, though..."

"What's that?" Gracie asked.

"You have to go to the beach real early and listen very close or...you'll miss it."

By now, Gracie was wondering if her long-time friend was okay. Still she was curious.

"So...what do you hear, exactly?"

"Oh, I hear lots of things. Sometimes, I hear Frank tell me he loves me. I miss him, you know. Other times I hear my mother read Bible verses, and then there's this voice, a friendly voice, that whispers things like, 'Never give up,' or 'You're not alone.' Things like that."

Gracie didn't know what to think about Rosemary's revelation so she decided to brush it off, for the moment anyway. It seemed to her that everyone was still stressed out because of Hurricane Matthew's recent visit.

Later, when all the club members had returned to the fountains at Coligny Plaza, Gracie asked Rosemary, "Were you serious about the sand whispering messages to you?"

Rosemary leaned her head back and roared.

"Oh Gracie, I was just pulling your leg."

Gracie glared expressionless for a moment and then laughed as well.

"Rosemary, you're a riot. You really had me going there for a minute."

Early the next morning, as Rosemary walked the beach, she saw Gracie at the water's edge.

That's odd. Gracie's a late sleeper. What's she up to? Then she noticed that Gracie's eyes were closed and her head was tilted as though she were trying to hear something.

Rosemary smiled.

I wonder...

Can you hear the sand whisper?
A message so true
With a kiss from the wind
It's meant just for you ...
Someone remembers
It's you whom they love
And why the stars watch
From high up above
As you listen intently
For a voice you once knew
Can you hear the sand whisper
When it whispers to you?

Lowcountry Off-Roading

Bill Newby

Once rice fields. Now waterfowl refuges.
Layovers for migrating flocks.

Dawn to 9:00 breakfast included.
No need for reservations.
Check-out as you wish.

We drive US 17 South
along the Carolina Birding Trail
and pull off at brown signs
leading to rutted dirt roads
over long-abandoned dikes.

From wildlife watchtowers
looking over the sheets of still water
and scatterings of resident ducks,
we hear the continuous hum of tires
spinning across the near interstate cement.

I ask the hostess at Skipper's Fish Camp,
"What's there to do in Darien?"
She replies in unedited certainty,
"Nothing! Just sit and enjoy the sun."

Natalie Nelson

Outdoors

Lisa Wilson

I smell the outdoors around me.
Pulling my shirt over my head,
I can smell the outdoors.

Working my long hair into a messy bun, I can smell it.
The smell of being outside.
The lingering memory of working the soil
remains on my hands.

The wind weaves the aroma all around me.
I can smell when the warmth
of the sun heats the earth.

The smell is home.

A Calling Card

Jeanne Silletti

Eager for some morning air and the arrival of the *New York Times*, I step outside and unexpectedly find a large, sturdy feather on my front porch mat. Stooping to retrieve this overnight memento, I ponder whether the feather was discarded during a flyover through the porch columns or resulted from a lingering respite on the wide floorboards. No matter, I welcome the gift.

Bird watching is a new pleasure. Displaced by a move to the South Carolina coast, I am comforted by the graceful beauty of the egrets, herons, and anhingas which inhabit the forest preserve and lagoon behind our home. Today's gentle encounter befriends and evokes a grateful heart. Smiling, I place the feather on my writing desk.

Jeanie Silletti

Taking a Side

John Barrett

Sandy Dimke

Beneath the Pines

Debbie Grahl

Hilton Head Island, 1911

Lightning flashed as the tall sea pines surrounding the old two-story plantation house swayed wildly in the rising wind. Ancient live oaks groaned and cracked as the sky darkened and the rain fell. Thomas Shelton stepped from the house onto the wide porch and peered into the darkness. Unable to see through the sheets of rain, he heaved the burlap and oilskin bundle over his shoulder and, raising his lantern, hunching into the wind, made his way through the sodden grass until he reached a thicket of trees.

Here, somewhat protected from the rain, he found the tree he was looking for and deposited his burden at its base. As he reached for the shovel he'd placed there earlier to mark the spot, a gust of wind almost knocked him off his feet. Around him branches snapped. He held onto the trunk of the tree for balance, praying he hadn't waited too long. In his forty years on the island he'd lived through a few hurricanes, but something told him that whatever was coming now was going to be horrific. But he'd had no choice. He had to wait until it was safe. The treasure had been in his family for nearly 150 years, and there were those around him he didn't trust.

He'd sent his few servants to the mainland and planned on rowing himself across the sound when he was done. As he began to dig, the wind died down, and the rain stopped. Other than the water dripping from the trees, everything around him went silent. Unease prickled the back of his neck as he shoveled out more of the sandy soil. Just a little further down and he'd be finished. A twig snapped behind him, and he whirled around, shovel held high. His eyes filled with surprise as a visitor entered the circle of lantern light.

"What are you doing here?"

The intruder smiled. "What do you think? I've come for what is rightfully mine."

"I have nothing that belongs to you, sir."

"I beg to differ. If I'm not mistaken, what you are in the process of burying," he tapped the sack with the toe of his boot. "Was stolen from my family, and I've come to reclaim it."

"We stole nothing from you. Samuel acquired these riches honestly. If your ancestors were careless enough to lose them, it is not my fault."

The intruder's face darkened with rage. "My ancestors were upright merchantmen. Yours were nothing but pirates and thieves. With the storm coming, I knew you'd either take it with you or bury it, so I've been watching."

Thomas kicked the sack into the hole. "Then, sir, you've been watching in vain." He lifted the shovel high. "For I will never relinquish my riches," Thomas yelled over the roar of the rising wind.

Torrents of blowing rain whipped their faces, and a mighty gust unbalanced both men. Thomas swung the shovel at the intruder's head, who ducked and lunged, slamming into Thomas, sending both men to the ground as a mighty crack sounded. They watched in horror as an eighty-foot pine tilted and came crashing down.

Hilton Head Island, October 2016.

Tears of relief filled Emily Hope's eyes as her VW bug rounded the curve and the house came into view. Even after the worst hurricane to hit the island in a century, the old plantation house still stood. As she had waited out the storm at her cousin Darla's in North Carolina, the reports had been sketchy. All she had known was that there had been structural damage, and thousands of trees were down.

She parked as close to the house as she could and stepped from the car. Petite, with chin-length blond hair and big brown eyes, Emily assessed the damage. Tall pines and live oaks lay everywhere, but none seemed to have landed on the house. Cautiously she stepped over fallen branches and piles of debris, slowly making her way toward the back of the house. As she rounded the corner, her heart sank. She hadn't been as lucky as she'd thought. A huge pine tree had crushed the roof of her screened porch. Emily sighed. Considering the destruction she'd seen driving across the island, only having a tree on her porch wasn't so bad. The rest of the property was another matter. How would she ever clear out all the fallen trees? Again sighing, she headed for her car. She'd unpack then begin looking up contractors.

As she crossed the wide front porch and unlocked the double oak doors with their beveled glass inlays, love for the house washed over her. When she'd first found the house three years ago, she'd known it was a place she could call home. Built in the 1850s, it was in need of some repair, but it seemed to call to her. Two stories with a four-columned porch, tall windows with wooden shutters, and a sweeping crushed oyster shell drive epitomized the Old South. Emily could picture ladies in hooped dresses fanning themselves while drinking mint juleps, horse-drawn carriages coming up the drive, and handsome men in broadcloth and straw hats sitting upon their horses. Always fascinated by images of the antebellum South, she'd quickly applied when she'd come across the job opening to head the Beaufort County Historical Museum.

Born in Boston, her father had been the owner of a fishing charter. One of Emily's first memories was the smell of the sea and the rocking of the boat. Her mother had loved to sail, and they'd taken their twenty-eight-foot sailboat up and down the coast. When Emily was away at college, her parents had been caught in a storm, and their bodies had never been found. She'd been devastated, but knowing what her parents would want her to do, she'd finished college with a degree in history. An only child, she'd sold the house in Boston and the fishing boat. Then, just before her twenty-fifth birthday, she'd accepted the museum offer.

Emily carried her bags up the curving staircase to her bedroom. She unpacked and headed to the downstairs study she used as an office. Thankful the power was back on, Emily set up her laptop and began to search for contractors. As she scrolled down the list, her doorbell rang. Frowning, wondering who it could be, she rose and headed for the door.

The man who stood on the porch took her breath away. Over six feet, he was lean but muscular. His hair was a rich dark brown and his eyes a smoky gray. Emily had to swallow before she could say, "Hello, can I help you?"

When he smiled, she thought she'd melt right there in the doorway. *For God's sake get a grip,* she told herself. *You've been alone too long.* Her friend Patty had been trying to get her to go out with a guy she knew at work, but since she'd had her heart broken a year ago, she hadn't been interested in dating. But if she was going to react like this when a good-looking man showed up at her door, perhaps she should reconsider.

"Hi, I'm sorry to bother you, but I saw your car and thought I'd stop. I'm Josh Campbell. I live up the road a ways. I see you have a number of trees down, and I wanted to know if you'd like help removing them?"

His southern drawl rolled off his tongue like silk, and Emily had to concentrate before she could reply. "Um, sure. Actually I was just looking up contractors. Do you have a tree removal business?"

He smiled and nodded. "My family does landscaping." He stepped back so she could see the logo on his truck. "I can help you with the debris. I can also cut up some of the trees to make it easier to remove them."

Emily finally had her wits about her and smiled back. "Mr. Campbell, please come in. You sound like an answer to a prayer."

As he walked past her, Emily couldn't help but notice how nicely his jeans fit.

"Would you like a soda or a beer?" she asked leading him into the kitchen.

"A beer sounds good." He glanced around. "What a great house. How long have you lived here?"

"Three years."

"Do you know the history?"

"A little. I did some research at the Heritage Library. It was a small Sea Island cotton plantation, but a few years after the Civil War, the owners went broke. It was purchased by a family named Shelton." Emily shivered and rubbed her arms. "I discovered that during the 1911 hurricane it's believed the owner drowned trying to row to the mainland. His body was never found, and the property was sold again. It's a little weird that I'm living here during another hurricane."

"Yes, but you're safe and sound."

Emily smiled. "You're right. So how long have you lived on the island?"

"Just a year. My dad retired and wanted me to take over this part of the business."

"Where did you live before?"

"Beaufort. That's where I grew up. I decided I didn't want to make the commute, so my brother took over that half of the business and I moved here."

"Well, if you can help me get rid of this mess, I'm glad you're here. Should we get down to business? How much is this going to cost?"

Josh laughed. "Don't look so grim. It's not as bad as you think. Actually I have a confession to make. I've seen you a couple of times but hadn't had the nerve to ask you out. So when I saw that I got back to the island before you, I walked around and assessed things."

For a minute Emily just stared. *Go out with him?* Did she hear right? Could the hurricane have brought her the man of her dreams? *Don't be a ninny. Go out with him.* "Ah, well, I'm not sure what to say," she stuttered.

He smiled. "Say you'll have dinner with me tonight."

Emily hesitated for only a moment. "Okay, sure."

Josh's smile widened. "Great. Here's the estimate for the tree removal." He slid a piece of paper across the counter. "See, it's not so bad."

The cost was very reasonable. She looked up at Josh and nodded. "You're hired."

"Great. If it's all right, my brother and I will be here first thing in the morning. Since the hurricane, he's been helping me out."

"No problem. I'm an early riser." She sighed. "Now all I have to do is find someone to repair the back porch."

Josh grinned. "Actually…"

Emily rolled her eyes. "Don't tell me, you're also a carpenter."

★ ★ ★

Emily awoke the next morning to the sound of chain saws. Recalling her dinner with Josh, she smiled. Only a few restaurants had reopened, and they'd gone to Local Pie for pizza. She couldn't remember the last time she'd enjoyed herself so much. *I'll invite him here to dinner tonight.* The museum was still closed, so she didn't have to go to work. She got out of bed and headed for the shower.

Because everything in the fridge needed to be thrown out due to the power outage, she'd go to the Piggly Wiggly and stock up. As she headed for her car, she noticed in the distance Josh standing in an area thick with fallen trees. Puzzled as to why he was working there, when trees closer to the house needed to be removed, she shrugged and started her car.

★ ★ ★

"This was a delicious dinner," Josh said, laying down his knife. "I might be from the Lowcountry, but there's nothing better than a good steak."

They sat in the kitchen alcove next to a large window overlooking the yard.

"Thanks, I'm glad you enjoyed it. I thought that since the house survived the storm, we should celebrate."

Josh took her hand. "The storm also brought us together."

Emily felt her cheeks turn pink. "Yes. Um, can you stay for a while? We could sit out on the porch swing."

He nodded. "I'd love to."

★ ★ ★

A couple of hours later, unable to sleep, her lips still tingling from his heart-stopping goodnight kiss, Emily sat in her den going through the stack of mail that had been delivered that day. A wide grin spread across her face when she opened the envelope from the ancestry site she'd sent her information to. Following along her family tree, she was surprised to see Hilton Head Island listed. She gasped in disbelief. According to the document, her ancestor, Samuel Shelton, lived in the area in the 1800s, and Thomas Shelton lived on the island in the early part of the twentieth century.

She shook her head in amazement, *Could I actually be living in the house of an ancestor who drowned during a hurricane? That would be way too weird.* She knitted her brows in thought. Her maternal grandmother's maiden name was Shelton, and all of mother's people loved the sea. Again she shook her head. No wonder she'd loved the house at first sight..

She glanced at the clock. Midnight. She'd lost all track of time. Yawning, she placed the ancestry papers in her desk, turned off the light, and headed upstairs.

Her mind jumping from Josh's kisses to the revelations about the Sheltons, Emily couldn't sleep. As the light from the full moon streaked across her bedroom floor, Emily thought she heard the sound of someone digging. Puzzled, she went to her open window and listened. Yes, it was faint but definitely digging.

She bit her lower lip. *Should I call the police? But what if it's just a night creature making the noise. I'll just go take a look myself.* She rolled her eyes. How many movies had she watched where some stupid female hears something in the basement and goes to investigate?

She cocked her head. *Are those men's voices I'm hearing?* She frowned. *It sounds like Josh. But what would he be doing out there this late?* Curiosity getting the better of her, she threw on clothes and headed down the stairs.

Quietly Emily went out the front door and made her way around back. The brightness of the moon helped her see, but also made her too visible. She ducked down behind some magnolias and strained to hear. It sounded like they were arguing, but she couldn't quite understand the words. She crept closer.

"Damn it, Jeremy, this isn't right. We should tell Emily."

"Why? This belongs to our family. She has no claim to it."

"It's on her land," Josh replied. "Besides, who knows if that old story is even true."

"Marcus Campbell died trying to get this back. It's been hidden for all these years. If it wasn't for the hurricane and the trees coming down, we would never have found it."

Unable to restrain her curiosity, Emily stepped from the bushes. "And what exactly have you two found?"

Josh, his face grim, stepped toward her. "Emily, please go back to the house. I'll explain later."

Emily brushed past his outstretched hand and gasped. There at her feet, lying in a pool of moonlight, was a human skeleton. "What in the world?" was all she could say.

"Emily, please go back to the house," Josh pleaded.

She narrowed her eyes and pointed to the other man. "Who is this guy, and what's going on?"

Josh sighed. "This is my brother Jeremy, and this," he said indicating the skeleton, "is Mr. Thomas Shelton."

Speechless, Emily looked from one man to the other.

"You might as well tell her," Jeremy said. "Then we can get on with it."

Giving his brother a sour look, Josh turned to Emily. "Supposedly a man named Samuel Shelton stole a fortune in gold coins from my ancestor. During the 1911 hurricane, Marcus Campbell confronted Thomas Shelton as he was burying the coins. The men struggled, and Thomas was crushed beneath a falling tree. Marcus, caught by the same tree, had his right arm and side severely injured. He made it home but only lived for a few days. Delirious with pain, he rambled on about coins buried beneath a tree on the Shelton land." Josh shrugged. "Before the hurricane this property was thick with trees and no one knew where to look."

Incredulous, Emily stared down at the skeleton, then turned back to Josh. "You're telling me gold coins are buried here? How did you ever find this spot?"

"When the live oak went down, its roots revealed the skeleton," Jeremy replied.

"You see, we kind of, um, scouted out your property before you got back on the island," Josh said.

"Yeah, and if you'd stayed away one more day, we'd have had the gold, and no one would have known."

Emily placed her hands on her hips. "Well, I'm here, and I'm calling the police. Gold or not, this was a human being, and the remains need to be collected and buried. In fact, I just found out tonight that I'm related to the Sheltons, so that makes me responsible for him."

Josh opened his mouth to speak, but Jeremy spoke first. "I don't care who you're related to, I'm taking the gold."

"We don't even know if the coins are here," Josh said.

"Whether they're here or not, I'm calling the police," Emily said.

"Emily, please, can we talk about this?" Josh asked.

Heartbroken over Josh's betrayal, Emily turned and began to run toward the house.

The force of the blow to her back sent Emily to her knees. Gasping for breath, she tried to rise. Then her head exploded in pain and blackness. As she lay semiconscious, blood trickling down her face, she heard Josh shouting.

"Jeremy, what the hell is wrong with you? You may have killed her."

"I don't give a damn. I'm not leaving without the coins."

"The hell you are."

Emily could make out scuffling sounds, then a sickening whack, then silence.

The next thing she knew, she was lifted and thrown onto someone's shoulder.

"Josh," she was able to mumble.

"No, your boyfriend won't be helping you," Jeremy sniggered.

Her head pounding and her stomach reeling, Emily forced herself to speak. "Where are you taking me?"

She heard him chuckle. "I saw a big gator in the pond on the edge of your property. I'll bet he'd like a midnight snack."

Panic shot through Emily. She tried to speak again but couldn't form the words. Jeremy tossed her to the ground. Water seeped into her clothes, and the smell of the marsh mud filled her nostrils.

"Don't worry, I'll make sure you're dead before I throw you in. You'll never know what happens."

Absolute terror revived her enough to plead. "No, please, don't. You can have the coins."

"It's too late. You know too much."

A scream lodged in her throat as he loomed over her. Then he fell sideways, landing half in and half out of the pond.

"Emily, are you all right?"

"Josh," she whispered.

He knelt beside her. "I'm so sorry. I had no idea he'd become so deranged."

Moonlight illuminated his blood-streaked face. "Josh, you're bleeding."

"He knocked me out, but my head is thicker than he thought. Here, let me help you up." As his arms went around her, they heard ripples in the water. Turning, horrified, they saw Jeremy's body being dragged into the dark pond.

"Jeremy!" Josh yelled, as he lunged for his brother.

Unable to speak, Emily watched as the alligator began to drag Jeremy under, Josh holding onto Jeremy's legs. When Josh's head went under, Emily screamed and stumbled to the edge of the pond.

"Josh," she screamed. Tears filled her eyes when he rose holding nothing but his brother's shoe.

Josh slowly made his way onto the bank and dropped to the ground. "I'm so sorry for putting you through this. Jeremy has been obsessed with the coins since he was a kid. And now look what it's brought him." Josh gulped deep breaths to calm himself.

"We need to call the police," he continued. "I'll take care of this and then get out of your life." He looked at her with such pain in his eyes. "He was my brother. I had to try to save him, Emily"

Emily's heart broke. She wrapped her arms around him. "I know. I know."

Another Day, Another Life

Sunni Bond

It just wasn't the same any more, Jackson thought. *Ever since the old man stopped coming to the games, it just wasn't the same.* Jackson had never said so, had never told him, but he admired that grizzly old guy. *What was his name? Oh, yeah, JW. Wonder what the "JW" stood for*—he had never said, and Jackson had never asked. Didn't really seem polite, and it didn't really matter what his name was anyway.

It hadn't rained in a month of Sundays on Hilton Head Island, as Jackson's grandmother was prone to say. The hard clay-packed yard seemed even harder than usual, if that were possible. There were cracks here and there, like old wood exposed too long to a baking sun. The humidity was high too, but it didn't seem to affect that packed clay.

Jackson didn't know why he kept coming to the games. He really ought to be looking for a job every day instead of spending his severance pay on the games. His Mama thought he was doing just that, but he had had so many rejections and no offers of a job that he had given up, at least for the time being. Maybe when the Super Wal-Mart came to the Island, he thought, then he'd find a job. Only problem was no one really seemed to know when that was going to be.

The big announcement hit *The Island Packet* months ago, and it had sounded as though the construction would start immediately. The weeks had gone by and become months, and not one indication of construction was evident around the current Wal-Mart. *I need to stop wasting time on whenevers and find something now,* Jackson thought. *I'm twenty two years old, time to be a man!*

Where was everybody else today? Had they changed to a different location and he hadn't gotten the memo? He'd give it a few more minutes, and then he'd head for home.

Then the cars slowly started arriving. First came Hootie in

his low-slung Thunderbird with Chaser riding shotgun. Those two always had money to bet, and Jackson had no idea where it came from, although he had a good idea it hadn't been gainfully earned. Pete and Mac on their motorcycles were close behind, and bringing up the rear was Harold. All of the arrivals were the younger members of the group, or "the young dudes" as JW had referred to them. Things had been a little uneasy ever since Angus had gotten picked up by the Bureau of Alcohol, Tobacco, and Firearms last month. There was something a little strange about that whole occurrence—only Angus had been arrested, and something just didn't seem right.

The older players didn't show up as regularly as they had previously, and Jackson felt as though the older men were not going to be much in evidence today either. He had first started coming to the games at the invitation of Clay, who was one of the long-timers in the group but even he didn't show up every time now. It was too bad; Jackson had always enjoyed the challenges the old man brought to the day.

Jackson drew a deep breath and crawled out of his truck. *Might as well get started*, he thought. Was this going to be his lucky day when he would walk away with more money than he had when the games started? Probably not. He wasn't very good at poker and that seemed to be the game of choice for most of the players.

He started across the grassless area toward the beat-up table under the shade of the live oak tree—and stopped. Lying propped against the tree was Simon, one of the young dudes, and he certainly didn't look as though he was simply sleeping. Nor did he look alive, come to think of it, and when Jackson spotted the spreading dark stain around the man, he knew the games would not be happening that day.

Pulling out his cell phone, he started to tap in 911, but Hootie snatched the phone away, screaming, "*What do you think you are doing?*" Jackson didn't see what the problem was—other than the dead man close by—in such a situation one called the authorities. What else did Hootie think Jackson could or should do?

Hootie told him in no uncertain terms that they couldn't afford to have the police come storming onto the property. He went on to say that they would have to dispose of the body they had just found and never talk of it to anyone. Jackson thought that was foolish talk, crazy talk indeed. To do such a thing made them accessories after the fact and subject to jail time.

Jackson had never spent any time in jail and he certainly didn't plan do so now. He grabbed his phone, holding on tightly to the device. Now everyone was shouting, talking about "who did this" and "how are we going to deal with it" and, worse of all, "where can we hide the body so it doesn't come back on us." Jackson eased himself away from the group as they all talked at once, each trying to be heard over the others. Sliding into the driver's seat of his Ford 150, he started the engine and pulled out of the yard without anyone really being aware he had left.

Now what? Jackson asked himself. *Who can I talk to about this,* he wondered. And then it came to him: *JW would know what should be done.* And he just happened to know where JW lived. Simply by chance, he had spotted JW's car in the driveway of a tidy house and yard just a few miles away one day when he was cruising around. Jackson pushed down on the accelerator and traveled the short distance as quickly as possible.

What if JW isn't home, thought Jackson; *what do I do then?* But that became a moot point when he saw JW sitting in the porch swing sipping on something tall and icy. JW seemed surprised to see Jackson but welcomed him onto the porch with a brief smile and a wave of his hand.

When Jackson had explained the situation at the site of the games, JW didn't say a word. He simply picked up his cell phone and tapped in a number. Jackson could tell it wasn't 911—too many punches on the keypad. Then he heard JW ask for Clarence, and soon he was explaining to the person on the other end of the phone just what Jackson had told him.

Jackson wasn't sure he had done the right thing, but he knew he didn't want to be involved in any kind of cover-up that those guys could conceive. He didn't understand why they were so against calling the police. Then Jackson remembered that some of them had served a little time behind bars; no big major crimes, but still jail time. And they would be the first to be suspects if the death of their fellow game player was determined to be foul play—and after all, what else could it be?

JW finished his call and put down his phone. "Young man," he said to Jackson, "you did the right thing. I want you to sit right here with me until we are sure that everything is taken care of." Jackson was willing to do that, but then he realized the others could try to pin the death on him. After all, he was the first to arrive at the game site; he had been there when the others arrived, and he had been the first to amble toward the table under the live oak. The others could tell the police he did it.

When Jackson expressed his concern to JW, the old man said, "That's why you're staying right here with me for the time being. I don't want you getting any more involved than you already are." Jackson didn't question JW's wisdom; after all, he had decided to come to the old man for advice and he might as well take it.

JW went inside the house and returned shortly with an icy glass of what looked like weak tea. "Arnold Palmer," said JW as he handed the glass to Jackson. "Huh?" asked Jackson—he knew Arnold Palmer was a well-known golfer but what did that have to do with a cold and refreshing drink? JW went on to explain that drink consisting of half lemonade, half iced tea was known as an "Arnold Palmer." Didn't matter to Jackson what it was called, it sure did taste good going down his parched throat.

After a while, a dark sedan pulled up in the yard. It looked like an unmarked police car to Jackson, but the man behind the wheel wasn't wearing a uniform. The man unbent his tall frame from behind the steering wheel, eased himself out of the car, stood and stretched, and then ambled toward the porch.

"Afternoon, JW," the man said in a voice that sounded like gravel being trod upon by heavy feet. Jackson thought he'd heard that voice before but he couldn't remember where. "Howdy,

Clarence," JW responded, "Can I get you something cold to drink?" The gravelly-voiced man thanked JW but declined his offer. Turning to Jackson, he asked him to tell him everything he remembered about the afternoon. As he did, Jackson noticed that the man did not take a single note, just listened with great intensity, never taking his eyes from Jackson's face.

When Jackson had concluded his narration, the man took a deep breath, nodded, turned to JW and said, "You did the right thing calling me, JW. This is just more of the same old story. Somebody got too big for his britches, so to speak, and somebody else wasn't going to let him get away with it. My problem is who took him out." Turning back to Jackson, he quizzed Jackson about happenings at the games the previous day and for several days earlier. Jackson struggled to remember everything that had happened during that time period but thought he gave a pretty good account of the time line and the events and the people involved. Nothing stood out for him as a cause for the death of his fellow gamer, but apparently it did for the man JW called Clarence. He nodded several times as Jackson talked of certain events over the past few days, and when Jackson had finished, he only had a few questions to ask.

Turning to go back to his car, Clarence stopped and turned back to Jackson. "I wouldn't go back there to play any games again, young man," Clarence warned. "You'd be better off just coming here to visit with JW, and I'm sure he'd enjoy your company." Then he turned on his heel as he gave JW a single nod and got in his car.

Jackson sat quietly for some time. Finally he looked at JW and asked the obvious question: "Who was that?" JW smiled and told Jackson that Clarence was the brother of his wife, Ella Mae. He went on to tell him that Clarence was a federal agent, and then Jackson remembered where he had heard that voice before: that time several months ago when the same big black car had wheeled into the yard where they were playing games and a new attendee who had tried to run away had been arrested and hauled away. No one else had been arrested, but Jackson remembered the words of the gravelly-voiced man telling JW to *"let it be"* when JW tried to pick up the cards and money when it had all scattered as the playing table was overturned. That was the last time JW had been at the games. And now Jackson thought he knew why.

"Can I come back to visit you again?" Jackson asked JW. "I think there are some things I can learn from you that will make my life better."

"Sure you can, son," JW responded. "Any time will be just fine." Jackson gave JW a nod and moved to his truck, pulling away slow enough so as to avoid causing the dust to rise and be a nuisance to the old man.

As Jackson pulled away, JW sat there in deep thought. Again picking up his phone, he punched in a number and when it was answered, he said "Ernest? This is JW. I think I've found just the young man you need for that vacancy you've got at your hardware store. Yeah, I'm sure he could come in to talk to you tomorrow or the next day. I think you'll really like him. Reminds me a bit of us when we were young, and you know that's a good recommendation right there." Laughing heartily at Ernest's response, he disconnected and leaned back in the swing.

Another day, another life taken away, and another life moving on, he thought. He just hoped Jackson wouldn't think he was interfering too much in his life. Somehow JW thought Jackson might turn out to be like the son he never had, and he had a feeling that Ella Mae would like him on sight. *Lord have mercy,* he thought—*she'll spoil that boy rotten.* But then he smiled again and thought maybe that wouldn't be such a bad thing after all.

End-of-War

Thelma Naylor

In a field,
overgrown with promises,
I search for end-of-war.

It's an unassuming herb,
you'd hardly ever notice,
clutching the earth, at
the feet of forget-me-nots.

Quite elusive
to mankind,
yet instinctive
for bees to find.

Should their buzzing
reveal a secret patch,
tend to it, make it spread,
throw some into the wind.
It may invade the world.

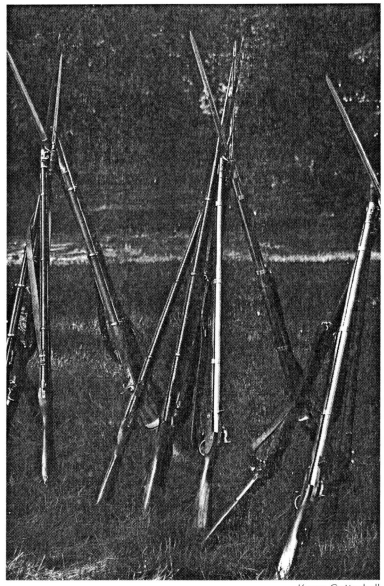

Karen Gottschall

Torn Between Two Gods

Greg Smorol

John Gunther was hosting the monthly family meeting in his formal dining room. William, John's brother, sat on one side of the table next to John's brother-in-law, Andy DuBois. The Gunthers' cousins, Paul and Joe Stobbs, sat on the other side of the table. Dinner was over and their wives excused themselves from the ensuing conversation.

John commented, "The maid has set up sweet tea and cakes on the veranda. It's a beautiful day. Time to let the men discuss business."

John had a snifter of brandy served to each man as he handed out cigars. The threat of impending war hung over the conversation like a fog.

They were in the town of New Castle situated in New Castle County, Delaware—smack on the Mason–Dixon line, which was between 1763 and 1767 to resolve a border dispute involving Maryland, Pennsylvania, and Delaware. They looked out the window and relaxed as they watched the Delaware River slowly flow past the house. The sight seemed to help to calm the tension building within them.

They were wealthy men, and each owned slaves. The difficult question they were about to debate was—would there need to be a war in order to keep their slaves? Owning a slave was a costly investment. When a slave was purchased, there was no guarantee that the slave would be useful enough to warrant that expense. Over time, the slaves that each of these men owned had been trained to be productive.

Losing their slaves would wreak havoc with the Gunther family finances. The Gunthers were planters. They produced a variety of crops, mostly grain, and shipped those crops to Philadelphia and the West Indies. Their profits depended on slave labor. Without that labor, the Gunthers would be reduced to being subsistence farmers.

It would be a hardship for the Stobbs. They owned several mills situated along Beaver Run, a tributary of the Brandywine River, in an area known as "the mill lands." They produced lumber, flax and paper. Their profits were good because of the slave labor. Some of their mills depended on low cost labor to make a profit, yet others could still make money with hired labor.

Andy DuBois had less of a problem as a dry goods merchant. Slaves added dollars to his bottom line, but he could get by without them if necessary.

John Gunther flushed as he spoke. "What's the problem with having slaves? We've all read the Holiness Code in the book of Leviticus. That's proof that slavery is allowed in the eyes of God."

Andy doubted that interpretation. "That's ancient history, John. These colored slaves are men, created equal like you and me. They've just had a bad lot in life."

William Gunther was perplexed as he replied to his brother. "I know we need the cheap labor, John, but if they're men, then we're paving ourselves a road to damnation."

Joe Stobbs couldn't let that argument rest. "They are not men like us. Their skin is dark. They can't reason like us humans. The Bible even says you can beat them when needed."

Joe's brother, Paul, disagreed. "What about old Henry? He's a Christian; sits in the back of the same church we go to. He can read and solve problems on his own. One of my best workers."

William chimed in. "Slaves in the Bible were men who sold themselves into slavery, or were war captives. They were shown respect and were treated with dignity. Ultimately they would resolve their debt and be set free."

Andy defined the conundrum. "We all go to the same church, but there seems to be two different Gods. John and Joe have a God full of fire and brimstone, while William and Paul have a God that is merciful and kind."

In an effort to avoid further confrontation, John changed the subject. "While you're all here, what do you think of our new silverware? We bought it in England when we went there to celebrate twenty years of happy married life."

Joe kidded John about the purchase. "Now you've set the bar at a high level. Our wives will expect the same when we reach that milestone."

Andy picked up a knife and read the name. "Eliza Godfrey. I heard she was one of the best silversmiths in England."

John beamed. "Right. This set belonged to the Duke of Cumberland. We'll keep it in the family forever."

It grew late as the men discussed how their businesses could complement one another. It was dark when they parted, fitting for the dark thoughts each man had on the possibility of an approaching war.

The next day John and William ran into a problem. William explained the situation to John. "Pete refuses to work today. He was attacked by a snake last night. He thinks it was a bad omen. He believes that if he leaves the house today he will die for sure."

John blew up. "What do you mean he refuses to work? He's a slave, he has to work. I'll handle this."

John grabbed his bullwhip and headed for Pete's cabin. He brought two other slaves with him and shouted out his command. "Pull Pete out of that cabin and tie his hands to the fence rail."

Pete railed in abject fear of the death his omen predicted. He was beyond reasoning. The two larger men could barely restrain him as they tied his hands down. They silently backed away.

John could see that verbal threats would not be enough to intimidate Pete in this condition, so he let the bullwhip fly. The braided rawhide left welts, and then tore open the skin. John stopped and asked Pete if he was ready to work yet, but Pete's fear was greater than his pain. The bullwhip struck again. Pete dropped to his knees.

William had had enough and grabbed John's arm. "Keep it up and you'll kill this man."

"He's a slave not a man. If he won't work, I don't need him anyway."

William walked over and untied Pete's hands. Pete fell to

the ground in silent agony. John glared at William, had second thoughts about continuing to whip Pete, and turned to head for home.

Life wasn't going well with the Stobbs brothers either. Paul had caught Amos, one of their slaves, stealing food. Joe was livid and took charge.

"What do you plan to do?"

"The hand that steals must go. It'll teach them all a lesson."

"You can't cut off his hand. He won't be able to work."

"Then I'll put him in the pillory for a week, with a sign saying this is what happens to a thief."

The pillory was in a place where all the other slaves, including his woman and newborn child, would pass by each day. He was barefoot and naked from the waist up. The sun scorched his body. He was deprived of food and given only enough water to keep him alive. At the end of the week he was hauled back to his cabin to recover.

The harshness of such punishments didn't sit well with William and Paul. They began to sit together in church to pray for their souls. William was worried. "Our slaves are humans, people just like us. We need to do something to convince John and Joe of this fact."

Paul had an idea. "Amos only stole food to feed his family. We weren't accounting for their new baby. What say we let Amos get married in the church with all the other slaves attending? Maybe our brothers will learn from that."

Both John and Joe thought it was a ridiculous idea, but the pastor had other opinions. "God doesn't want mankind living in sin. A marriage is the rightful manner to handle this situation."

Paul made sure that Amos and his bride were properly dressed for the wedding. He even gave them wedding rings. William had food prepared for a reception in the church yard to celebrate the marriage.

At the reception, Paul and William mingled with the slaves and wished the couple a happy marriage. John and Joe sauntered around the fringes of the crowd discussing the event. Joe was irate. "Look at all that good food wasted like that. I don't know what's wrong with Paul. I don't seem to know him anymore."

John agreed. "Same thing with William. I'd step in and do something about it, but the slaves are working better than ever. I've got the whip ready for when that changes."

In the following days, John and Joe found solace with one another in the back row of the church. They continued looking up and referring to passages in the Bible that supported their beliefs about slavery. They saw no need to be remorseful for their actions. Merciful handling of slaves was not in their character; they were disgusted with their brothers' soft-hearted mannerisms.

On a larger scale, the nation's North and South were becoming increasingly belligerent towards one another. Talk of secession had started, and the strengthening of the military had begun.

When Abe Lincoln, running as a Republican in favor of banning slavery, was elected, seven cotton-based slave states formed a Confederacy. Other states soon joined them when they seceded from the Union. On April 12, 1861, Confederate forces fired upon Fort Sumter, and the Civil War began.

John Gunther and Joe Stobbs immediately enlisted in the Southern army. As John said, "These slaves are my property, and if I have to fight to keep them, then so be it."

William, Paul, and Andy joined the local militia and prepared to protect their families and town. When fighting broke out at Sewell's Point, the war seemed too close for comfort. Then the Battle of Aquia Creek convinced the townspeople to take action. They melted down the church bell, along with some scrap iron, and had two cannons made.

New Castle had the river protecting its back. The easiest way to attack it would be from the long draw to the South. The local militia decided to place a cannon on each side of the draw to spread out the firepower. They also built a low wall to provide protection for their infantry. William and Paul were trained to fire the cannons. Andy would help load them and direct fire. They stockpiled powder and canister shot and waited for the war to come to them.

Bigger battles were being fought elsewhere when John and Joe were given command of a troop of infantry. They knew the area and were told to secure the towns and gather supplies for the army. New Castle was in their sight. They didn't expect much resistance. They brazenly marched up the draw when the cannon fire rained down on them. The canister shot spread out its shrapnel and wiped out swaths of marching men. John yelled out, "Drop back to the woods; we need to refigure our attack.

Joe was shocked. "I don't know where they got those cannons, but I can't imagine them having much ammunition. Let's make some fake charges and get them to use up their ammo. Then we'll move in from the sides of the draw and overtake their position."

Joe and John had their men make several short forays that drew cannon fire as expected. At first, the cannons fired at every charge, taking few casualties. Gradually the cannon fire became more sporadic and the charges were stopped.

Joe felt the plan had worked. "They must be nearly out of canister shot. I say we attack early tomorrow morning."

John agreed. "Good plan. I'll lead half the men up the left side; you take the others up the right."

William, Paul and Andy weren't experienced fighters. Andy saw the troops retreat. "These cannon were a fine idea. The Rebs ran away."

Paul wasn't so sure. "I think they'll regroup and come back. How much powder we got?"

William checked. "We got a lot of powder, but not so much canister shot left. A lot of the canisters were confiscated when our army passed through."

Paul was worried. 'We need to keep these cannon firing or their experienced soldiers will make short work of us. Send out a group of men to collect any pieces of metal we can use to build our own canisters."

Andy went house to house asking for small pieces of metal for the cannons. He sternly commanded each family to comply with his order. "You must put anything you have in a sack and leave it on your doorstep for the militia to pick up."

At John Gunther's house, Pete was given the task of filling the bag. He gathered bits and pieces of metal around the carriage barn before going into the house and collecting any tableware, nails, screws, hinges, and whatnots he could find.

Andy collected the sacks and made canisters that were added to the ammunition supply. Paul had them set to the side. "We don't know how well these homemade canisters will work. We'll save them for last."

Andy was in command of firing the cannons. He ordered a few more rounds to be fired at what he thought were attacks, and then announced their problem. "We're out of canister shot. Load up the home made shot and hold fire. We'll wait until they reach the top of the draw before firing again."

At dawn, two lines of men began pouring out of the woods and running up the sides of the draw. William knew his riflemen were no match for the soldiers below. "Half of you get on either side of the rampart and hold your fire. When we fire the cannons, pick off the lead men, but don't shoot until you're sure you can hit them."

On the Rebel side, John and Joe felt their plan was working. They led their men up the sides of the draw without any resistance. Joe cleared the top first. John saw the cannon fire rip Joe and his men apart. He turned his attention back to his own charge when the cannons fired at him. He felt several pieces of shrapnel hit him as he fell to the ground. He watched his men being picked off by rifle fire. There was blood spouting out of his upper leg where an artery had been severed. He felt a hole in his stomach where shot had passed through him. He only had a few minutes to live when he noticed something that seemed familiar imbedded in his shoulder. He pulled it out. It was a fork, a piece of cutlery. He read the inscription—*Eliza Godfrey*.

Kajieme Powell Is Dead

Jim Riggs

He strolled into the store. Helped himself to sport drinks.
Then, the man returned. Stole pastries. Confronted the clerk.
Kajieme Powell was shoplifting.

Two cops responded. Cops in a cruiser.
He's big! He's black! He has a knife!
Kajieme Powell's a threat.

He's pacing; walking toward us. Stop or we'll shoot!
Shoot me. Shoot me. Shoot me now.
Kajieme Powell's suicidal.

I know the guy. He's mentally ill. It's a paring knife.
Doesn't matter. He's walking toward us. Too close.
Kajieme Powell's aggressive.

Stop! Drop the knife!
He's too near. We aren't safe. Shoot!
Kajieme Powell's unresponsive.

Bang! Bang! Bang! Bang! Bang! Bang! Bang!... Bang! Bang!
Oh my God. They just killed this man. He's dead. This is crazy.
Kajieme Powell's lying on the sidewalk.

Oh, my God. They could have tazed him.
They could have shot him in the leg.
Kajieme Powell had to die.

He was aggressive. He was armed.
The man was emotionally disturbed. He wanted to die.
Kajieme Powell's dead.

The man was black. He was a thief.
The world was watching Michael Brown.
As Kajieme Powell fell dead.

Kajieme Powell lies in another pool of blood.
His shooters cuff the corpse. As the world watches Ferguson
Kajieme Powell lies dead.

Donna Varner

Coincidental Timing

Bill Newby

The return address had an embossed lettering that felt pebbly under his touch. It looked clean and crisp, giving a prestigious aura to the smooth white envelope. *Office of Graduate Studies.* This is it, he thought. He held it in his hands a moment longer, feeling its heft, nothing more than a single page inside—not another round of brochures and forms. Just the word.

Beth would be as eager as he to discover what it contained. Earlier that morning, looking up from the paper, a buttered bagel at her lips, she'd sighed, "I wonder when we'll hear whether you're in or out. Jeff asked me yesterday if he should look for someone to replace me this summer, and I didn't know what to tell him. All this waiting's driving me crazy."

Still feeling the polished grain of the envelope, he glanced at the rest of the mail in the box. A Sears mailer in comics-page hues; a blue envelope with a golden portrait of a saluting marine in full dress uniform; and another phone bill. Fortunately, their security deposit should cover this one.

Climbing the stairs, he thumbed through the Sears mailer. Men's shirts, belts, and shoes.

How does anyone buy shoes from a catalogue? If you didn't like them, would the company pay for the return postage?

"Yes, that's right, I'd like to keep this pair, just for the month. Please send me the next larger size for comparison, and if you have anything similar in brown I'd like to see that as well."

Women's slips, bathrobes, washers, dryers, refrigerators, and fans; then camping equipment —his favorite section, but what god-awful products. Coolers, lanterns and sleeping bags that all would weigh a ton. It's ludicrous to think anyone could camp while hauling these things around. Maybe they should find another term for this section–travel gear, road-side roaming, something else, but not camping. Camping was lakes, portages, rapids, and mosquitoes. No one in his right mind would lug a Coleman Cooler into the wilderness. You might do that if you had an outboard and a cabin, but that was summer cottage living, not camping.

At the third floor he unlocked the apartment door and dropped the catalogue in the wastebasket. They weren't about to make a trip to Sears, but it was comforting to know that American businessmen still viewed them as potential customers.

The newspaper still lay on the table when he entered the kitchen. "5th Battalion Arrives in Cam Ranh Bay" ran a headline over a picture of troops carrying duffel bags as they deplaned from the belly of a transporter with its tongue on the ground. The picture was unavoidably crisp and almost bleached with brightness. Eyes squinting in the noon blaze. Heat shimmering off the tarmac.

He pulled down on the refrigerator handle, a vertical spear of opulent chrome, and the huge, Buick-bulked door swung open. A wave of cold air greeted his face and arms as he pushed the milk carton aside and slid out the pitcher of orange juice. Thank God for Lawson's truck drivers. The nearest orange grove must be an easy thousand miles away, but it would be hard to get through a day without a citrus injection, that pulpy, sour liquid sunshine. Even in the north country he'd begin his days stirring orange crystals in a cup. No pulp, lots of sugar, but that slightly sharp taste that would enrich the cool morning as mist lifted off the still water. What about those troops in Vietnam? Did "C-rations" mean citrus? Was it even C, or was it K?

Glass in hand he went back to the living room and plopped down on the couch, trying not to dislodge the red and black throw that Beth had picked to enliven the dirty olive green of the furnished sofa. Yes, they had done a lot, especially she, to try to bring some life into this cramped space. Setting the glass on the table, he remembered their candlelight dinner two nights ago. Pasta was cheap, and even he could throw a green salad together.

There might not be a lot of money, but with each other's love they could easily compensate.

Getting married young had been a strain on both of them. On her own, Beth could easily have found a graduate program in anthropology. She'd graduated magna cum laude, and having been Dr. Richardson's lab assistant and protégé during her last two undergraduate years would have opened many doors. In fact, it had taken several forceful confrontations on her part to keep Richardson from sending unwanted letters of recommendation to the Browner group at the University of Arizona. A perfect opportunity for Beth. Incan ruins high in the Andes. A team of energetic researchers who had often collaborated with Richardson. But no, she said their marriage was too important. There would be plenty of time to dig up the past. Life was for the living, and it had been a joy living with her.

Two nights ago, they'd sat on that couch and had their meal together. Beth shared stories of Jeff's frustrations with the newest waitress, but what a dear he was, and how he wouldn't fire anyone during the first week just because they'd dropped a whole platter of main courses. And as they laughed together and sipped Chianti, the candlelight gently caressed her cheek and put a gleam in her eye. Afterward, as he took off her slip, and slowly stroked his hand over her soft, delectable curves, the candlelight continued to enhance her beauty and their lovemaking. It always ended, but in the midst of it he felt as though he could nestle in her warmth and beauty forever.

But no, soft candlelight gave way to TV glare, capping their evening with the nightly news as they had been doing almost daily throughout the past year. With a mix of interest and obligation they had subjected themselves to the unraveling horrors. Body counts. Troop movements. Viet Cong attacks. A riveting televised nightmare bathing their nakedness in stark black and white and leaving them silent, distant and alone.

Now, sitting in the beam of sunlight across the couch, he picked up the white envelope and held it squarely, reading his own name, printed in crisp, clean letters–clearly the work of a disposable carbon ribbon in a high-priced typewriter. He could see the secretary, not some grad assistant or roving member of a typing pool, but a conservative, polished professional in an attractive suit, precisely positioning and errorlessly typing his name. After all, one would expect no less from such an institution. Quality academics—quality throughout.

Glancing back at his name he found himself repeatedly voicing the syllables within his mind, and he thought of his brothers, sisters, and father. Were his father there with him, across the room, he would be sitting with a proud smile and an eager lean. Yes, his dad would take great joy in seeing his first son take another giant step in academia. His dad didn't fully understand that scene. He hadn't completed college himself and didn't readily comprehend what it meant to roam the library stacks and to try to spend one's life in three different centuries, not to mention one's own. But he did value accomplishment. And he knew, without any doubt, that higher degrees came from hard work, represented high status achievement, and opened many high-level doors. Yes, his father would be proud. One of his was making the grade.

The Depression and World War II had kept his father from completing college. The events of the day were just too powerful to contradict. But it was hard to grasp his father being rejected by the armed services, supposedly for bad eyesight. Sure he wore glasses, but wasn't that true of nearly half the world? Hell, his father could see just fine, and he always seemed physically fine as well.

They used to go out on the expansive front lawn late on Saturday afternoons and throw a football to each other. His father could rifle a bullet pass thirty-five yards that would hit him on the chest one count after he turned to receive it. How they could ever turn down a man like that he would never know. But at least he was rejected. He knew there was a need, offered himself, and was told to help in some other way. Stay home and contribute to the war effort through industry. Keep the assembly lines cranking. The war can't be won with soldiers alone.

He set the white envelope aside on the table and looked at the blue one with the golden salute. His name was also displayed there, on a slip of white paper pasted a bit off-center and on a slant. Obviously a purchased mailing list. Probably one of the ways the university attempted to make ends meet.

He looked at the soldier and studied the face, strong-jawed, clean-cut and confidently alert. Not a real face. Just some artist's rendition of an idealized warrior. The same face the artist would have placed on the shoulders of Charlemagne or Nelson.

But then he saw that other face, the one that had been unexpectedly popping into his mind's eye over and again during the last four months—Tommy's uplifted face winking at him across the huddle as they all put their hands in the middle and psyched themselves up for the second half.

Tommy was almost always laughing. Life was just a game to him, and he was so talented that every obstacle was simply flavoring, spice, something to improve the meal. Like being double-teamed. He loved it. His jump shot was so quick, his release so high, there wasn't a single defender in the league who could hold him below thirty points. Scoring was so easy, it was almost boring. But when they double-teamed him, it brought out his best. It was then that he and everyone else knew what a joy it was to be alive.

All those years with Tommy came back to him with a rush. The snap of a wet towel in the showers after a game. Double-dating, pizzas, first beers, talking about the future.

How did it happen? When they had gone off for college, their paths had parted, and one thing led to another until they were out of touch. And then, just that past Christmas, when he and Beth had gone to his parents, he had picked up an "Alumni News" sitting on the kitchen counter, flipped to that section dealing with his class, and read, "Lieutenant Thomas R. Klausner, U. S. Army, killed in action while serving his country in Vietnam, October 3, 1968." He could hardly believe it. Tommy. He just stood there, stunned, and then closed the magazine, set it back on the counter, and in a daze found his way to an armchair in his old bedroom where he sat in somber silence for the rest of the afternoon. Tommy.

Beth had called up the stairs with that compellingly playful voice, urging him to join the sledding party that was just forming and that would be leaving in ten minutes, but he begged off. And even when they made love later that evening, he felt hollow and spent most of the night staring into the darkness.

He picked up the blue envelope, flipped it over, slid his finger beneath a corner of the flap, and broke the seal. It was a form letter from a recruiting office on Wacker Drive, congratulating him for graduating—"an accomplishment of which you should be proud." It stated that as a college graduate he was "an excellent candidate for a leadership position in the defense of our country" and that it was far better to enlist in officer training with the Marines and to "serve with distinction among the most elite fighting force in our nation" than to allow his Selective Service Board to determine his fate. It closed with a "Please feel free to call on me" message from a Sgt. Melvin Rhodes.

His Selective Service Board would probably eat up graduate studies. Sure the nation needed soldiers and field commanders, but they didn't seem to be having any trouble filling their quotas. Another professor/researcher in the making would probably satisfy everybody, and there was a part of him that yearned for that life. Roaming the stacks might be something his father would never really understand, but he did. There was a whole world, many worlds, sandwiched on those bookshelves, and with time one could savor them all.

He refolded the letter, slipped it back into its blue casing, and set it back on the table. He reached across the white envelope and felt the cool moisture on the glass as he raised it to his lips and took a long swallow. Liquid sunshine!

Beth had never been to the woods, and as they had talked about the possibilities of the summer to come, one of their dreams had been getting a week away, driving north, and camping together.

There could be nothing better—orange crystals, mist, and Beth. But out of that golden salute Tommy continued to wink at him, and he knew that it might never be as they had dreamed.

Enough. He finished the glass, picked up all the mail, and went to his desk, a door with legs, that sat across the room from their bed. He put the telephone bill in the "Pay" clip and then pulled out his copy of "Harrison's Complete Shakespeare." He wedged the white envelope firmly against the inner binding, in the middle of the second act of *Hamlet*, closed the book and slid it back into its place. She'd never look there, and he could pull it out whenever he was ready. One way or the other, he hoped they could talk it through, together.

His radio clock said one-fifty. The train was just two blocks away. He should be able to make it to Wacker Drive by three.

Anatol Zukerman

Who's There?

Anatol Zukerman

Chained to a mid-size planet
in an endless space full of flying rocks
our hearts expand and contract
pulsating away like our big universe
and knock on the cage of our ribs:

Knock-knock! Who is there?
No answer.

Parrots repeat our questions
and laugh at our endless quests.
They know there can be no answer
but we don't listen to stupid birds.
We know: someone must be there!

Knock-knock! Who is there?
No answer.

We writhe under doctors' knives,
go on diets and exercise
in order to live in this magic place
a little bit longer.

We make our children and gods
in our own image, divide the world
into friends and foes, we go to wars
and kill each other to prove our worth.

Knock-knock! Who's there?
No answer.

We cry at the end: Let's do it again!
We are sorry, we can do better!!

Knock-knock! Who IS there???
No answer.

Yet Another If-I-Had-Life-to-Do-All-Over-Again Poem

Barry Dickson

First, I would shut up more.
I discovered one cannot talk and learn at the same time.
Oddly, I *could* talk and listen. But it would always be me
I'm listening to. And never once, in all my life,
did I ever hear myself say something I didn't already know.

This time I will not leave the hospital early the day my mother dies
just because I'm feeling fidgety. I will be there when she goes,
to say good-bye to someone who thought
all my ideas brilliant, all my jokes hilarious
and "Warren Beatty and Brad Pitt could only wish they had such
a face."
Most of us don't get more than one of those in a lifetime.

Speaking of which, this time I will not let Lucinda Gluck go
because I thought her ultimatum was "too soon."
Too soon for what, Barry? Too soon to be loved?
Too soon to have a best friend for life?
Too soon to go to bed every night with the smartest,
most beautiful woman in northeastern Pennsylvania?
Clearly it wasn't too soon to be an asshole.
And if she ever reads this, I will be mortified.

That's another thing I will do this time around: be mortified more.
This business of not doing because of what might happen
creates a life lived in place. Before life can go somewhere good,
it first must simply go. Like Yogi said,
"We're lost, but we're makin' good time."

Donna Varner

Family Transportation

〜

Jeanie Silletti

Our tired and rusted Hudson sedan was abruptly traded for a new, 1959 Volkswagen bus, an extraordinary purchase for an oversized family of undersized income. All of our belongings were second hand, so family discussions about buying a brand new car excited each of us. As the eldest daughter and one grown used to voicing an opinion, I eagerly suggested we buy a sleek, wood-paneled Ford station wagon much like my friends' parents drove. My recommendation was promptly ignored.

The next day I returned home from school, to a large navy VW bus with an unfinished interior blatantly parked in front of our house. Outraged, my Irish temperament flared, and my teen-age tears flowed. Patiently my kind father tried to reassure me that while station wagons were fine for some families, we needed more capacity. He reasoned that this VW with its three bench seats and raised rear luggage shelf would be perfect for the ten of us. I argued in vain that he should also have thought about appearances . . . station wagons were what "normal" families drove. I felt singled out and publicly embarrassed every time I entered and descended this bus posing as our family car.

Sundays were the worst! Mother loaded her Catholic brood into this camper and Dad, head held high, drove us to church like we owned a Cadillac. On arrival, I felt the critical gaze of my best friend, Barbara, as one brother after another tumbled out of the side doors while the youngest two children were retrieved via the hatchback door. After this circus I entered the church humiliated. Composure took some time, but after encouraging words from my father, I silently prayed to St. Jude, Patron Saint of the Impossible, to help me make peace with this vehicle.

I suppose it wasn't until I turned 16 that I became painfully aware that if I ever wanted to drive, it was this monster or nothing. One bold day, with my Dad lending technical assistance, I got in on the driver's side, put the car in first gear, and drove the unfashionable VW down our street.

Many decades have passed since that first test drive. Today, I drive a beloved, five-speed, leather interior, cream-colored VW Beetle. Curiously, I frequently recall with fondness and good humor my youthful days behind the wheel of "the bus."

The Price of Coral

Elizabeth Robin

Turn white and die!
such a catchy slogan
might amuse, if stark truth
awakened alarm or purpose

yet we flock to watch our victims
four thousand years in the making
the gentle rainforests of the sea
living in elegant algal symbiosis
inhabit a sliver and foster an ocean
one marvel spotted even in space

would that coral turn its stinging cells
on us, squeeze us in its tentacle rings

a snorkeling wonder
teeming diverse delight
now a pale shadow
as ocean bottoms blanch

and we deny, deny, deny swimming
one stroke closer to a color-free world

a licensed vendor stops by with a case
of cheap beads and coral bracelets
pinks and reds--no white here
even our jewels reek of murder

Open Water

Miho Kinnas

The annual 3.2-mile river swim in Beaufort, South Carolina

No rope. No line. Water is water but I am home alone. With thousands of strokes, kicks, and breaths, I stitch together six bright yellow balloon buoys. Bacteria, fungi, algae, decaying spartina cling on. I count nothing but the strokes. After twenty, I look up. I survey. Earlier, I saw a dolphin swimming into the marsh. The Beaufort Memorial on my left. The complex keeps changing its shape. An optical illusion. White magic. I finally extricate myself. from its presence. All I hear are my own splashes and a groan with every exhale. The anchored luxurious boats are stubbornly stationary on the calm morning water. A paisley-shaped island is hidden behind them. Numerous piers jet out from waterfront gardens like the minute hands of train-station clocks. A green capped swimmer catches up with me. But I don't let him pass me. The blinding sun blurs the terminal point.

Open water.

Open life.

The InSide Info

Linda O'Rourke

Contributors

R. Elliott Anderson has a B.S. in journalism and an M.A. in political science from the University of Illinois-Urbana-Champaign. He worked for the General Electric Company and as a management consultant based in Cambridge, MA. His feature articles have appeared in the New York Times, Reader's Digest and other newspapers and business publications. A piece on debit cards was featured on CNBC and NBC Nightly News. He and his wife Arlene are Hilton Head Island residents.

Will Anderson earned a Doctor of Science degree from MIT, served as an army captain, and spent 29 years with NASA. He retired in 1995, and he and his wife moved to Hilton Head. His three action-adventure novels draw on his knowledge of aerospace systems, piloting and related experiences, relationships, and travels. The novels, *The Anomaly*, *Missiles in Space*, and *Armed and Counting Down*, can be previewed at willandersonweb.wordpress.com.

Dianne Appell, an award winning, exhibited and published photographer, feels honored to have had her work chosen to appear in the IWN's fourth and fifth anthologies. "I love the editing, post-processing phase of photography. Today's familiarity, or mastery, of complex software editing programs combined with one's vivid imagination, can produce exquisite results. Nothing, however, tops the appreciation and recognition of my efforts by others, both in and out of the field." dianneappell@gmail.com

FranBaer is active in Hilton head's Camera Club, Audubon Society, and Carolinas' Nature Photography Association. Birdwatchoing is a primaryhobby. and she helps in conservation functions for Audubon. uing her camera to document birds in two ongoing surveys on Hilton Head Island. She enjoys exhibiting her work, and images have won many ribbons in competitions. Somr have been published locally in calendars, books, newspapers, and magazines (including *BirdWatching* and *South Carolina Wildlife*)

Judy Law Barnes (1943-2015) created the charcoal portrait of Rhett and Scarlett in 1993 while living in Charelston, before her move to Hilton Head. She enjoyed road trips to New England and points out west. Judy's path was filled with a generous spirit and immense talent that tickled the hearts of all she met.

Sunni Bond is a returning author to the IWN anthology. Her story in this issue is a sequel to the previously published short story in *Time and Tide*. Previously published works have been in the non-fiction field in such publications as *MENSA Bulletin*. A retired teacher (business and social studies) who is currently an active genealogical researcher "just for the thrill of the chase," she enjoys helping people connect to their ancestors.

Len Camarda is originally from NY City, but his business career took him around the world, inluding living in Panama, Holland and Spain. His time in Spain inspired his published novel, *The Seventh Treasure*, an international thriller rich in history. "Matthew's Socks" is Len's fourth publicantion in IWN's anthology series. He is an accomplished painter and exhibits at the Art Gallery of Coastal Carolina in Shelter Cove. See Len's work at www.lencamarda.com.

Tom Crawford has published three books since retiring to Hilton Head from a career in journalism with the Worcester (Mass.) *Telegram & Gazette,* UPI and the Springfield (Mass.) *Republican. Foibles* is a collection of humorous and self-deprecating essays. *Goli Otok (Naked Island)* is a Balkans novel based on his stint as a foreign correspondent based in Belgrade, Serbia. *Resurrections...of an Obituary Writer* contains obituaries and essays about the most influential and/or memorable personalities of his news career.

Barry Dickson is a retired Creative Director on Madison Avenue, where he worked thirty-five years. His poetry has appeared in a variety of journals, print and online, including *North American Review, PEARL Literary Magazine, New England Journal, HazMat Literary Review* and his favorite, *AsininePoetry.Com*. He's been a finalist for the Hearst Poetry Prize and received a *Pushcart Prize* "Special Mention." His work covers a wide range of subjects from relationships to politics to cheeseburgers.

Sandy Dimke enjoys creating art from the natural world around her. After spending 20 years in architectural photography in Connecticut, she now resides in Beaufort. An active member of Carolinas Nature Photographers and a founder of the Photography Club of Beaufort, she is currently the Director of the International Club Print Competitions for the Photographic Society of America. She has published two photography books, and her art has appeared in numerous books and magazines.

Suzanne Eisinger was raised in Illinois and went on to obtain her bachelors and graduate degrees from Arizona State University and Ithaca College in New York, respectively. Besides Hilton Head, her adventures have taken her to California, Wisconsin and Virginia. Formerly a Speech Pathologist, she now spends her time keeping track of two teenage boys and a tween daughter, freelance writing and community service. Her articles regularly appear in *The Daily Press* of Hampton Roads, Virginia and on www.Kveller.com.

Marty Ferris retired from teaching and then visited South Carolina's low country and became captivated with its natural beauty. Three years later, Marty is knee-deep in a first novel, *The Lost Pearls*, set in the barrier islands of South Carolina and Georgia.

Karen Gottschall's love of the outdoors and travel has provided many unique photo opportunities. Her images have won local competitions in several states and on-line forums. A resident of Okatie, Karen is the current (2017-2018) president of the Photography Club of Beaufort and has coordinated speakers and workshops for several area photography clubs.

Debby Grahl's first release, *The Silver Crescent*, won the Paranormal Romance Guild's 2014 Reviewers' Choice award. Her latest book, *Rue Toulouse*, a contemporary romance set in New Orleans, was a finalist for the First Coast National Excellence in Romance Fiction Award and was a choice read by *Hilton Head Monthly*. Visually impaired since childhood, she uses screen-reading software to research and write her books. She enjoys murder mysteries, time travel, and, of course, romance. See www.debbygrahl.com and www.facebook.com/debbygrahlauthor.

Judy Groves, a native of Tennessee, has loved writing song lyrics, poetry and fiction since eighth grade. After several years as a Realtor, she decided to study technical and creative writing at Pellissippi State College and is now doing what she loves: writing full time! In addition to her participation in *Ebb and Flow*, she is currently seeking a publisher for *Redemption on Third Street*, and a children's book, *The Adventures of Detective Shelly*.

Bev Moss Haedrich's work has appeared in Beaufort and Charleston magazines, Chamber of Commerce publications, and newspapers. Her local travels encourage others to discover the joys, serenity, and fragility of the Lowcountry, a place she has lovingly called home for thirty years. She writes fiction and nonfiction, and encourages others to journal their journey. Her favorite quote is 'All those who wander are not lost.' She can be reached at bevsletterproject@gmail.com.

Charlie Harrison practiced General Surgery in Bryan, Ohio for thirty-three years until his retirement in 2006. He began taking writing classes on Hilton Head, found them stimulating, and has continued to write with valuable advice and encouragement from other writers. His only published piece is an essay regarding the rewards of teaching medical students. He writes, when inspired to, for his own enjoyment.

Rachelle Jeffery started her photography "career" in 8th grade when she was given her first camera. Even though she considers photography her hobby, she has won many awards in camera club competitions. She enjoys photographing everything and anything that catches her eye. Rachelle is currently a member of the Camera Club of Hilton Head. Taking photos goes along with her motto "Do what you love and love what you do."

Miho Kinnas is a Japanese writer and translator. Her book of poems is *Today, Fish Only* (Math Paper Press 2015). Her poems appeared in *Quixoteca: Poems East of La Mancha* (Chameleon Press 2016), *The Classical Gardens of Shanghai* (HKU Press 2016) and other online literary magazines. She translated haiku for *Equatorial Calm* (Celestial 2016). In 2017, Miho conducted haiku workshops through Shanghai International Literary Festival and Pat Conroy Literary Center. She holds an MFA from City University of Hong Kong.

Norm Levy's long career in advertising taught him the value of compressed communication leavened with a smidgen of humor. He is the author of *Rhymes for Our Times*, a book of rhymed riffs on real news headlines calculated to amuse and to occasionally instruct. He is also a published blues and country western song writer, active on social media, and a proud contributor to the four previous Island Writers' Network anthologies. www. rhymes4ourtimes.com

Ann Lilly has lived her entire life in the South. In 2001 she moved from Lexington, Kentucky to Hilton Head with her husband and two daughters following a career in accounting. She's been an active Realtor on the island since 2004. Ann has been writing for many years and recently published her first children's book, *Scoot's New Home*, an illustrated story about a little boat living on Hilton Head. Several of her stories were in IWN's 2015 anthology, *Time & Tide*.

Phil Lindsey graduated from Illinois State University with an accounting degree in 1976. In 2016, he retired full-time to Bluffton, SC, and is attempting, through poetry, to exercise the right side of his brain. His poetry spans a wide range of subjects, including light-hearted childhood memories, comical parodies, and human mortality. This is the first time his work has been selected for an anthology, but you can read more of his poems on www.Hellopoetry.com.

Carol Linneman is a Registered Nurse with an MSA Degree and Graduate Gerontology Certification. Having worked and studied in long-term care settings and personally experienced nursing home life as a supportgiver, Carol offers assistance to other supportgivers through her guides and talks. Publications include *Personalizing the Nursing Home Experience, From Caregiver to Supportgiver* (via Amazon), and customized guides for specific group needs. Her creative non-fiction short stories, uniquely showcasing local volunteer opportunities, appear in magazines and respective websites. www.supportgiver.com.

Marilyn Lorenz is a graduate of Northwestern University. First published at the age of sixteen, her prose and poetry have appeared in national magazines and journals as well as all five of the Island Writers Network anthologies. "Great Blue Gert," her children's picture book, sold out in one year and is now a Lowcountry collector's item. "Everyone in my family is creative," she says. "It's what we do."

John "Mac" MacIlroy, a former attorney, CEO and adjunct professor, lives along a Carolina tidal marsh with his wife, a painted ceramic dodo bird named DuMont, and a pesky mortgage. In addition to writing short fiction, he has coauthored a book, *Not Exactly Rocket Scientists and Other Stories* (www.NotExactlyRocketScientists.com), released July 2017 – a collection of zany, "mostly, mostly true" stories. Pat Conroy called it "a great book about friendship."

James A. Mallory is a freelance writer and editor who relocated to Hilton Head Island in 2015. He is a retired newspaper executive with 30 years of management, editing and writing experience. He retired from *The Atlanta Journal-Constitution* as Senior Managing Editor/VP News. He writes fiction and non-fiction and is currently shopping a detective mystery centered in his hometown of Detroit.

Duncan McPherson found his passion for photography in college, spent many late nights in the darkroom at Virginia Tech's architecture studio. Photography's unique blend of art and science resonated with his desire for creative expression and precision. After graduation Duncan moved to HHI to work for an architecture firm and now lives in Asheville, NC where he practices architecture and often points his camera at the mountain landscape.

Sansing McPherson, an Alabama native, taught writing from middle school through college. She joined the Island Writers' Network in 2002 upon moving to Hilton Head Island from New Jersey. She has served on five editorial boards for IWN's anthologies and has short stories in each. Her novel, *Sweat Sisters*, is set in a New Jersey middle school. *Kirkus Review* praised it and featured it in a March 2017 issue. www.sansingmcpherson.com

DJ Murray put her artistic desire on hold while raising the family but returned to it as a dedicated artist. Her works received awards at juried shows and are shown at SOBA gallery and the Art League of Hilton Head gallery. She trains daily as a competitive swimmer having held some top 10 times in the nation in the distance events. During some long workouts colors flash through her head which inspire her for some of her paintings. 78

Kendra Natter is an active member of the Camera Club of Hilton Head Island and chairperson for the Kurtzberg Awards which challenges and recognizes local High School photographers. Kendra's work has been featured and recognized in competitions at CCHHI, Tri-Club Events, Osher Life-Long Learning Center, Coastal Discovery Museum and the Art League of Hilton Head Island. Kendra is a Photography Instructor at the Art Academy of Hilton Head Island.

Thelma Naylor enjoyed an international upbringing as the daughter of a Foreign Service officer. Degrees in Languages and Linguistics from Georgetown University allowed her to globetrot as an interpreter and contribute to computerized translation and other natural language applications. With her husband Bill, she retired to Hilton Head in 2000. Thelma has dabbled in poetry and short story writing since 2015, with pieces published in IWN anthologies and *The Breeze*.

Natalie Nelson moved from Michigan to Hilton Head Island in 1988. As a Michigan school administrator in a rural district, Natalie shot photos of sporting and school events for the district newsletter. She has worked with professional photographers editing, shooting conventions, private events and weddings. Now retired, Natalie pursues her passion for shooting landscapes, flora, and fauna. Viewing her images you will see her passion for images that catch your eye and touch your soul.

Bill Newby moved to Hilton Head from Cleveland, Ohio. He worked as a high school English teacher, department head and administrator and as a college of education advisor and lecturer. He uses poetry and fiction to record and explore moments of celebration, complaint, concern and comedy. His work has appeared in *Whiskey Island, Ohio Teachers Write, Bluffton Breeze, Sixfold, Palm Beach Poetry Festival Fish Tales Contest,* and IWN's *Time and Tide*.

Gretchen Nickel bought her first digital camera enroute to Peru in 2007. From then on she was hooked and passionate about photography, seeking the unexpected in her travels, valuing composition and detail. She loves settling into a new place and really getting to know it as opposed to being a tourist. A resident of the Lowcountry for just three years, Gretchen has fallen in love with the intoxicating marsh aroma of her new home!

Linda O'Rourke, originally from New York, has lived in several areas of the US. When Linda retired from the banking industry in Chicago, she and her husband relocated to the beautiful Lowcountry area. She loves to travel and developed her photographic eye in the world's arena along the way freezing moments in time as images. Linda's work has been published in local publications and books and is included in Camera Club of Hilton Head Island Exhibitions. You can see more of her images at <u>lindaorourkephotography.zenfolio.com</u>.

Lindsay Pettinicchi loves taking pictures of nature and wildlife, scenery and landscapes, and commercial and architectural photography. Most of her Hilton Head Island nature and wildlife photos were taken while biking on her beautiful island; moving targets are her favorite subjects. Her 2017 recognitions include the *South Carolina Wildlife Magazine* - Hampton Wildlife Fund Photo Contest, The Connecticut Audubon Society Our Natural World Photo Contest, and eleven top finishes in several Connecticut agricultural fairs.

Susan Proto launched her photographic career with a Brownie camera. There have been many starts and stops on her journey as she pursued a business career while raising her family. Only in 2017, as she entered retirement, was she able to fully focus on her photography, including being an active member of HHI Camera Club & HHP Artists Association, plus showing her work at the Twenty/20 Café, the HHI Library, the Bluffton Library & the OLLI Center.

Jim Riggs published his first novel, *Freedom Run*, in 2015. A career mathematics teacher, he earned his BA from Iowa State Teachers College and MA from Northwestern Oklahoma State. He spent many of his retired years as a professional nature photographer, and shortly before his retirement, began writing poetry and stories of his family history. Jim enjoys writing nonfiction and poetry, but loves fiction the most. Two new novels and several short stories fill his time.

Elizabeth Robin retired after thirty-three years teaching high school English. She enjoys a second career as a writer on Hilton Head Island. Her first collection of poems was published by Finishing Line Press in 2017. *Silk Purses and Lemonade* explores the challenges of the human experience, both personal and cultural. A second chapbook, *Where Green Meets Blue*, will be published by Finishing Line Press in early 2018. See more about her poetry, non-fiction and fiction at http://www.elizabethrobin.com.

Jeanie Silletti is a retired community college faculty member who taught classes in cultural anthropology in Ohio prior to her 2015 move to Hilton Head. Her background also includes twelve years of European residence (Spain, England and Italy) and international teaching experiences. Today, she continues her interest in education in Savannah where she is an art docent with the Telfair Museum. Jeanie enjoys writing, especially vignettes about growing up in a large, Irish family of ten.

Greg Smorol received his Baccalaureate Degree from St. Lawrence University in Canton, New York, and a Masters Degree in Communications from SUNY at Buffalo. He has published short stories in several IWN anthologies and has a novel, *The Tithonian Biosphere*, currently available on Amazon. He and his wife Donna reside on Hilton Head Island.

Norma Van Amberg is a retired, award-winning journalist. A graduate of Douglass College, Rutgers University in her native

New Jersey, she has lived in the Hilton Head Island–Bluffton area since 1984. She worked for *The Island Packet* as a staff writer from 1985 to 1997 and as editor of *Coastal Sport & Wellness* until May 2010. She is a NAMI Lowcountry Board Member and is polishing her non-fiction book about mental illness.

Cynthia Van Nus was a former resident of Michigan until moving to Hilton Head Island in 1999, whereupon, she continued her career in psychotherapy. Since retirement in 2015, Cynthia has focused on her art interests, mainly photography and fine art painting. She is a member of the Camera Club of Hilton Head Island and the Society of Bluffton Artists. Cynthia's main focus is photographing and painting landscapes, seascapes, and other nautical scenes.

Donna Varner's photographs reflect her unique eye, her sense of design, and her way of seeing the world. Donna has enjoyed taking pictures since childhood and learned photography as an adult through workshops, books and experimentation. She has augmented her artistic sensitivities by taking courses in drawing, painting, collage, printmaking, clay and book arts. Donna exhibits at arts festivals and juried shows, and shows her work at Pluff Mudd Art in Bluffton, SC.

Terri L. Weiss is a part-time Hilton Head resident. A Georgetown Law School alum, she is a Fellow of the American Academy of Matrimonial Lawyers and listed in Best Lawyers in America. She is currently working on her second novel, *Book of Genesis*. Her short stories include 'Somerset' (Monadnock Writers Group, *Shadow and Light - A Literary Anthology on Memory*, November 2011) and 'By Order of the Synod' (2012 Pikes Peak Writers Fiction Contest, prize-winner). Her website is http://terrilweiss.com.

Lisa Wilson earned a Master's in Public Administration from Drake University. She currently resides in Iowa but longs for beach life. Lisa is passionate about writing but only recently put pen to paper writing poetry and short stories.

Gene Youtz has been doing research on life for over 75 years, of which 50 were spent in the Washington, D.C., area in printing and publishing. He produced work for business, non-profits, and professional associations for 50 years, then retired to pursue his true love and began writing his *Newslessletter* for the Internet. He and his wife Barbara, a watercolorist, live on Hilton Head (with summers off to the Maine Coast) where they prepare words and pictures for presentation.

Anatol Zukerman, an unfortunate man, graduated from Harvard School of Design to begin sweeping floors in a factory. He traveled the world to find a good word and to live in a perfect democracy. He committed no crime except writing in rhyme, and he quit his profession in time to be happy in his own company. He's a builder and bard, and he worked very hard to get into this IWN anthology.

About the Island Writers' Network

When writer Jo Williams moved to Hilton Head Island in 1999, she missed her Charlotte, NC, writers group, so she ran an ad in the *Island Packet*. Eighteen people responded, and twelve attended the initial meeting. Since then the Island Writers' Network membership has exceeded fifty active members, over two dozen of whom are published, either with traditional publishing houses or e-publishing companies. The Heritage Library has been IWN's gracious host through the years.

Notable alumni include Kathryn Wall, author of the popular Bay Tanner mystery series with St. Martin's Press; Vicky Hunnings with three mysteries by Avalon Press, and Dee Merian, whose memoir, *The Best Years of Flying* (Headline Books), appeared at Book Expo America in New York in 2010. Currently active writers are Brian Thiem, former Special Ops Marine and swat-team cop with an MFA in writing, with three hit Matt Sinclair thrillers; award-

winning romance writer Natasha Boyd with a recently released and highly praised historical novel, *The Indigo Girl.*

IWN has three meetings a month: a business/program meeting on the first Monday of each month, excepting July and August, at 7:00 p.m. at the Heritage Library, 852 William Hilton Parkway, Hilton Head Island; Open Mic on the third Monday, including July and August, at 7:00 p.m. at the Heritage Library; and Last Wednesdays, a coffee house format with readings and music at a local restaurant, at 6:30 p.m.

IWN aims to encourage and mentor writers of all levels both in the craft and business of writing. Members work in all genres including fiction, non-fiction, children's literature, humor, memoir, and poetry. The group has published four previous anthologies: *Hilton Head Island: Unpacked and Staying* (2007), *Hilton Headings* (2009), *Living the Dream* (2012), and *Time and Tide* (2015). All are available at Amazon.com and at several local vendors. Check IWN's website for current meeting schedule, vendors, and events. www.islandwritersnetworkhhi.org.

About the Cover

Robert Ovelman - Professional Photographer

Bob's love of photography began in high school with a box camera. He believes that photography has not changed much since then. It is still seeing the picture with your eye, capturing it and saving it as a lasting, visible image. He takes a photojournalistic approach to photography – telling a story without using the written word.

After graduating from Virginia Tech with a Master's degree in Architecture he served in the Air Force as a pilot in the Strategic Air Command. When he left the Air Force he practiced architecture, concentrating on transportation - airports and railroad facilities.

He became the corporate photographer for Amtrak and freelanced as a photojournalist for several newspapers.

He photographs worldwide—people, nature, architecture, and any subject which tells a story. He has been a guest lecturer on cruise ships and teaches photography, helping others to become "the complete photographer" by using their imagination, creative skills, and composition techniques. His photographs have won many national and international awards. He won the Ritz Camera Company national competition grand prize two years straight. The Philadelphia Camera Club named him Photographer of The Year, and his photographs hang in the State of Delaware Governor's office, the United States Senate Office Building, and in the private collections of several prominent people. bobovelman@aol.com.

Index